Scripture Discussion Commentary 12

SCRIPTURE DISCUSSION COMMENTARY 12

Series editor: Laurence Bright

Last Writings

Hebrews *Lionel Swain*

Pastoral epistles *Jerome Smith*

Revelation *John Challenor*

ACTA Foundation

Adult Catechetical Teaching Aids

Chicago, Illinois

First published 1972
ACTA Foundation (Adult Catechetical Teaching Aids),
4848 N. Clark Street, Chicago, Illinois 60640

Nihil obstat : John M. T. Barton STD LSS *Censor*
Imprimatur : + Victor Guazzelli *Vicar General*
Westminster, 5 July 1972

Library of Congress number 71–173033

ISBN 0 87946 011 3

Made and printed in Great Britain by
William Clowes & Sons, Limited
London, Beccles and Colchester

Contents

General Introduction   *Laurence Bright*   vii

Hebrews   *Lionel Swain*   1
Introduction   3
Plan of the letter   7
Book list   8
1   Prologue   *Heb 1 : 1–4*   9
2   Excellence of the christian revelation   *Heb 1 : 5–
    2 : 18*   13
3   Exhortation to faithfulness and confidence
    Heb 3 : 1–5 : 10   21
4   Subject and purpose of the letter   *Heb 5 : 11–
    6 : 20*   27
5   Excellence of Jesus' priesthood   *Heb 7 : 1–28*   30
6   Excellence of Christ's high priestly liturgy and
    mediation   *Heb 8 : 1–10 : 18*   33
7   Exhortation to faithfulness and other virtues
    Heb 10 : 19–12 : 28   41
8   Epilogue   *Heb 13 : 1–25*   47
9   General conclusion   50

The pastoral epistles   *Jerome Smith*   53
Introduction   55
Book list   58

v

1   Timothy's task   *1 Tim 1 : 1–20*   59
2   Order in the church   *1 Tim 2 : 1–3 : 13*   71
3   False teachers, and pastoral practice   *1 Tim
       4 : 1–6 : 2*   86
4   Conclusion to 1 Timothy   *1 Tim 6 : 3–21*   102
5   The work of the ministry   *2 Tim 1 : 1–2 : 13*   107
6   False teaching   *2 Tim 2 : 14–4 : 22*   117
7   The letter to Titus   *Tit 1 : 1–3 : 15*   128

Revelation   *John Challenor*   137

Introduction   139
Book list   143
1   Letters to the Asian churches   *Rev 1 : 1–3 : 22*   144
2   Events before the end   *Rev 4 : 1–16 : 21*   152
3   The fall of Rome and the defeat of evil   *Rev
       17 : 1–20 : 15*   171
4   The new Jerusalem   *Rev 21 : 1–22 : 21*   179

General Introduction

A few of the individual units which make up this series of biblical commentaries have already proved their worth issued as separate booklets. Together with many others they are now grouped together in a set of twelve volumes covering almost all the books of the old and new testaments—a few have been omitted as unsuitable to the general purpose of the series.

That purpose is primarily to promote discussion. This is how these commentaries differ from the others that exist. They do not cover all that could be said about the biblical text, but concentrate on the features most likely to get lively conversation going—those, for instance, with special relevance for later developments of thought, or for life in the church and world of today. For this reason passages of narrative are punctuated by sets of questions designed to get a group talking, though the text of scripture, helped by the remarks of the commentator, should have already done just that.

For the text is what matters. Individuals getting ready for a meeting, the group itself as it meets, should always have the bible centrally present, and use the commentary only as a tool. The bibliographies will help those wishing to dig deeper.

What kinds of group can expect to work in this way?

Absolutely any. The bible has the reputation of being difficult, and in some respects it is, but practice quickly clears up a lot of initial obstacles. So parish groups of any kind can and should be working on it. The groups needn't necessarily already exist; it is enough to have a few like-minded friends and to care sufficiently about finding out what the bible means. Nor need they be very large; one family could be quite enough. High schools (particularly in the senior year), colleges and universities are also obvious places for groups to form. If possible they should everywhere be ecumenical in composition: though all the authors are Roman catholics, there is nothing sectarian in their approach.

In each volume there are two to four or occasionally more studies of related biblical books. Each one is self-contained; it is neither necessary nor desirable to start at the beginning and plough steadily through. Take up, each time, what most interests you—there is very little in scripture that is actually dull! Since the commentaries are by different authors, you will discover differences of outlook, in itself a matter of discussion. Above all, remember that getting the right general approach to reading the bible is more important than answering any particular question about the text—and that this approach only comes with practice.

Volume 12 contains three very different writings, all probably produced towards the end of the new testament period. Hebrews is a strikingly original piece of theological writing, Revelation a uniquely Jewish-flavoured piece of apocalyptic, and the pastorals represent the rather humdrum life of the church as it settled down towards the end of the century.

                                                        L. B.

Hebrews

Lionel Swain

Introduction

Nothing certain is known about the exact identity of Hebrews' author, its date, its addressees or the precise circumstances in which it was written. From the fourth century in the West, and even earlier in the East, it has been commonly attributed to Paul, but its literary characteristics and theological tempo are, on the whole, so markedly different from those of the genuine Pauline letters that this view is untenable from the critical standpoint. Nevertheless some connexion with Paul is very probable. It could have been written by one of his close companions or fellow missionaries, possibly even on his instructions. This hypothesis would explain both the mention of Timothy in 13:23 and the affinities which it has with Paul's letters. Since it exhibits an acquaintance with Paul's captivity letters it could hardly have been written before these, say 65, and since Clement of Rome used it about 95 it must have appeared before this date. The maturity of its theology also suggests that it is one of the latest writings of the new testament. The absence of any mention of the fall of Jerusalem or of the destruction of the temple is a possible—but not certain—indication that it was written before 70. The shadow of this impending disaster might well explain the allusions to God's imminent judgement and suggest a Palestinian destination. The title 'to the Hebrews' did not belong to the original document and was probably added in the second century. The letter's contents suggest that it was originally addressed to christians of Jewish background who were very familiar with the old testament and its cultic institutions and were able to appreciate the author's peculiar method of argument which is a curious and ingenious combination of the allegorical exegesis associated with Philo of Alexandria and the techniques of the Palestinian rabbis. Thus 'Hebrews' describes them most aptly. They also appear as second generation christians who have grown lukewarm, apathetic and indolent in their commitment to Christ and are in danger of missing their final goal. But it is not evident either that they are ex-Jewish priests tempted to revert to judaism or that they are threatened by a bloody persecution. The mention of Italy in 13:24 could be a clue to the letter's place of origin, which would corroborate its link with Paul. Despite all the obscurity about his identity, the author of Hebrews was certainly a literary genius second to none of the other new testament writers. With the possible exception of Luke, he has produced the most polished Greek in the new testament. Paradoxically, his mentality and style are more semitic than hellenistic and it has been suggested that the letter in its present form is an accomplished Greek translation of a Hebrew or Aramaic original. His method of argumentation is concentric rather than linear and at the end of the work the patient reader has the distinct impression that he has traversed the same ground several times. Like astronauts in a lunar module orbiting the moon many times in order to acquire a complete coverage of its surface from different angles, he repeatedly returns to the same subject, each time zooming in to concentrate on one of its facets. Thus the work must be viewed as a whole, each of its parts being considered as harmoniously combined with the rest, rather like a Beethoven symphony or Renoir painting. However pregnant or profound a particular phrase or text may appear in itself it conveys the meaning intended by the author only in so far as it is seen in relation to the whole work. This demands a great deal of attention and patience on the reader's part. A work of art, Hebrews is to be contemplated rather than merely read. In fact it is probably the most exquisitely constructed of all the new testament books. It certainly was not produced in a day. The author has clearly taken great care to select and collate different sources, possibly from his own teaching, preaching and apologetics, and has welded them together with all the well known literary devices, such as the concentric structure, chiasmus and inclusion, to form his masterpiece. The major contents of Hebrews may well have circulated in an oral form before they arrived in their present context.

It is impossible to classify Hebrews into any one category of literary genre. Apart from the last chapter which contains an epistolary conclusion and strikes a more personal note, it has none of the characteristics of a letter properly so called. Elsewhere, it appears variously as an oration, a homily, a theological treatise or an essay in biblical exegesis. The author himself calls it a 'word of exhortation' (13:22) and, given the dominant note of exhortation throughout the whole work, this is probably the best overall description. It is an exhortation which absorbs other different literary genres and, being sent to a given community or group, has the character of a letter or 'epistle'.

This observation concerning Hebrew's literary genre, together with the remarks about its composition and structure, provide the indispensable key to its proper understanding. They show that the author's aim is directly pastoral rather than doctrinal or theological. True, Hebrews is not surpassed in doctrine and theology by any other new testament writing, and indeed is richer in these than most. The Father's initiative and primacy in redemption, its trinitarian structure, the divinity of Christ, his priesthood and sacrificial death, the new covenant, the liturgical character of the christian life, the priesthood of the faithful, the pilgrim church, faith, hope, the definitive character of the christian revelation, the inevitability of God's judgement, the power of his word, the impossibility of a second repentance—these are only the major themes which occur, some of them only in Hebrews or more clearly than elsewhere in the new testament. Nevertheless all this doctrine and theology appear not for their own sake but in order to serve the author's main purpose: to exhort his readers, by promise or by threat, to rise from their stupor and complacency, to renew and intensify their original commitment to Christ and to press on courageously to their final end. Unless the reader views Hebrews in this perspective he risks grossly misunderstanding the author's message. This applies particularly to what is undoubtedly Hebrew's most original and characteristic doctrine, Christ's priesthood. As important and as developed and 'mature' as this theme is in Hebrews it is still subordinated to the author's main intention. He does not mean to elaborate a theology of Christ's priesthood. Rather, adapting himself to his readers' background and mentality, he presents Christ the high priest with his self-sacrifice as an example of faithfulness, a source of comfort and encouragement and a basis of hope. It is impossible to extract from Hebrews a fully developed theology of Christ's priesthood. Neither should the author's assertions be quoted without regard for their original context. The plan and the equilibrium of the whole work must be respected. The author must be allowed to speak for himself.

Of all the new testament writings, with the possible exception of Revelation, Hebrews is the most enigmatic and disconcerting for the modern mind. Nevertheless the reader who has the patience to unravel its message will be more than rewarded by a vision of the christian mystery which is perennial and transcends the time, circumstances and culture in which it was first presented.

Plan of the letter

1. 1:1–4   Prologue
2. 1:5–2:18   Excellence of the christian revelation
    (a) 1:5–14   The Son and the angels
    (b) 2:1–4   Exhortation to take God's word seriously
    (c) 2:5–9   The man Jesus and the angels
    (d) 2:10–18   Incarnation and priesthood
3. 3:1–5:10   Exhortation to faithfulness and confidence
    (a) 3:1–6   Jesus and Moses
    (b) 3:7–4:11   Exhortation to faithfulness
    (c) 4:12–13   The incisiveness of God's word
    (d) 4:14–5:10   Exhortation to confidence
4. 5:11–6:20   Subject and purpose of the letter
    (a) 5:11–14   Reprimand for immaturity
    (b) 6:1–8   Exhortation to maturity
    (c) 6:9–20   Encouragement and exhortation to hope
5. 7:1–28   Excellence of Jesus' priesthood
    (a) 7:1–10   Melchizedek and Abraham
    (b) 7:11–28   Melchizedek's priesthood and the levitical priesthood
6. 8:1–10:18   Excellence of Christ's high priestly liturgy and mediation
    (a) 8:1–5   Heavenly priesthood and sanctuary
    (b) 8:6–13   Mediator of the new covenant
    (c) 9:1–10   The liturgy of the old covenant

(d) 9:11–14   Christ's liturgy
(e) 9:15–24   Christ's mediation
(f) 9:25–28   Christ's unique and definitive self-sacrifice and second coming
(g) 10:1–4   Inefficacy of the law's sacrifices
(h) 10:5–10   Efficacy of Christ's sacrifice
(i) 10:11–18   Efficacy of Christ's priesthood and mediation
7. 10:19–12:28   Exhortation to faithfulness and other virtues
(a) 10:19–31   Exhortation to sincerity, faithfulness and love
(b) 10:32–39   Encouragement and exhortation to confidence and perseverance
(c) 11:1–40   Excursus on faith
(d) 12:1–11   Exhortation to shun sin and to persevere
(e) 12:12–13   Encouragement
(f) 12:14–17   Exhortation to virtue
(g) 12:18–24   Sinai and Sion
(h) 12:25–29   Exhortation not to neglect God's word
8. 13:1–25   Epilogue
(a) 13:1–19   Exhortations
(b) 13:20–21   Blessing
(c) 13:22–25   Final exhortation, personal news and blessing

Book list

The Jerusalem Bible.

The *New Catholic Commentary on Holy Scripture*, Nelsons 1969.

The *Jerome Biblical Commentary*, Chapmans 1969.

F. F. Bruce, *The Epistle to the Hebrews*, Marshall, Morgan and Scott 1965.

1

Prologue
Heb 1:1–4

In these first four verses the author gives a very succinct and dense résumé of the message which he will expound throughout the whole work.

God the Father has the initiative in redemption, which is here seen primarily as his revelation, his self-disclosure in the person of his Son made man, thus demanding, of its very nature, a response on man's part. God began to reveal himself within the history of the Jewish people and he has brought this process to completion in Christ. Despite this manifest continuity, however, the christian revelation transcends infinitely that made to the fathers and which is implicitly styled 'old', both as far as the prophets (1:1) and the law (1:4) are concerned. The prophetical revelation was successive, partial and varied, whereas the christian revelation is complete, unique and decisive, occurring at the end of time. Right from the outset, therefore, the author lays the basis for his insistent exhortation: to the absolute finality of God's word in Christ there must correspond an absolute commitment on man's part.

The christology of the prologue serves to underline the excellence of the christian revelation and it is a veritable *summa* of the new testament's faith in the person and work of Christ, comparable with the prologue of the

9

fourth gospel and the hymn of Col 1:15–20. The term
'son' is polyvalent and could refer to a Jewish king, the
Jewish messiah, a just man or even an angel. The author
dissipates all obscurity on this point by modifying it with
the ideas of heredity and mediation in creation. The son
is depicted as heir, not simply of all nations as the Jewish
king and messiah of Ps 2:8, but of the whole universe.
He is the end of creation. Further, in terms evocative of
Prov 8:22–31 and Sir 24:9, he is described as pre-existing
creation, since the Father made the world through him.
In 1:3–4 the author repeats the thought of 1:1–2, expressing an even more profound christology and providing a
more panoramic view of the mystery of redemption.
Christ is the Son of God in the fullest and most unique
sense of that term since, although being distinct from the
Father, he is the most complete expression of his being
and exercises the divine prerogative of the government of
the universe. He is thus the revelation of the Father in
person (Jn 14:9) and there can be no further, more complete revelation. God has nothing more to say after Christ.
It follows necessarily that the christian era is in 'the last
days', the end of the world. The movement of the author's
thought is denoted by the tenses of the verbs in these
verses. From the consideration of what the Son *is*, the
author moves on to what he *has done* and then to what
he *has become* and obtained. The thought structure is
strikingly similar to that of the christological hymn in
Phil 2:6–11, following the whole movement of the incarnation and redemption, from the pre-existence and
divine nature of the Son, through the incarnation, passion and death, to the resurrection and heavenly exaltation of Christ. The movement ends where it began, with
a change, not in the Son but in the human nature which
he has assumed, since it has now been introduced into the

divine sphere. The author thus sees three stages in the work of redemption: Christ's divine sonship, his priestly work of purification and expiation, his heavenly enthronement. For the author Christ is son, priest and king, but, since the idea of sonship is introduced to underpin the transcendence of the Father's revelation, he is also prophet or, more precisely, revelation itself, the word of God. This view represents a remarkable interpretation of certain old testament passages in the light of the Christ-event, especially Wis 7:25–26, Ps 2:7–8 and Ps 110:1, 4 whereby Christ is seen as wisdom incarnate and the transcendent fulfilment of the Jewish messianic expectation. In particular, the event of Christ's passion, death and resurrection inspires the author to connect verses 1 and 4 of Ps 110. In its original setting the psalm speaks of a Jewish king or the messiah, who enjoys a royal priesthood, with no explicit mention of a specifically cultic or liturgical function. The author has it from tradition that Christ entered his glory through his passion and death (Lk 24:26). His originality consists in reading this schema into the text of Ps 110: it was by his priestly act of expiation for sins (1:4) that Christ has taken his seat at God's right hand (1:1). In contrast to the messianic king who exercises a priesthood after his enthronement, Christ's royalty is the fruit of his priesthood. The paradox is that the one person who *is* Son of God by nature (1:3) should *become* Son of God by his passion, death and resurrection (1:3–4), but it is precisely in this that redemption consists. The unique Son of God, in becoming man, has assumed human nature, and by the ascension has introduced it into a new, divine existence, so that henceforth all men might have a new 'way' open to them, the possibility of becoming sons of God in the Son of God: the Son became man so that men might become the sons of God. Thus the process of communication with man which God began in the old testament reaches an undreamt of and unsurpassable climax in Christ's paschal mystery. The circle is complete: God has spoken to man in his Son and the Son has spoken to the Father in man.

The introduction of the idea of angels in 1:4 serves both to counteract any tendency to subordinate Christ to the angels or to identify him with any one of the heavenly powers, as was quite fashionable in some gnostic circles, and to emphasise the superiority of the new covenant over the old which, according to some Jewish traditions, was mediated on Mount Sinai by angels (Gal 3:19).

How does the prologue sum up the doctrinal teaching of the whole work?

2

Excellence of the christian revelation
Heb 1:5–2:18

(a) Heb 1:5–14. The Son and the angels

The author now proceeds to develop the topic which he has just introduced: the Son's superiority over the angels. He does this, in typical rabbinical fashion, by accumulating several passages of the old testament which he considers to prove his thesis. Since this is the first time that we have met the author's explicit use of the old testament, and since it forms a major part of his work, it will be useful to consider at this point how he understands and uses the old testament. The Christ-event, although occurring within our spatio-temporal order, ultimately transcends the grasp of the human mind. However much it is scrutinised, understood and explained, it will always be wrapped in a penumbra of unintelligibility. This involves that it can never be fully understood and expressed in the thought-patterns of any one culture, including the Jewish culture shared by Jesus himself and his first disciples. The christian faith cannot be deduced from, nor reduced to, an ingenious exploitation of old testament ideas. The Christ-event is utterly unique. The new testament does not grow organically out of the old, rather the revelation of Christ marked a radical break with judaism

13

on many points. Nevertheless, the very first christians, being themselves of Jewish origin and imbued with the literature of the old testament, naturally had recourse to it in order to grasp and explain to their contemporaries the mystery of Christ which had been revealed to them at pentecost. In this they followed the example of Jesus himself. The fact that the christians of subsequent generations have been able to discern a neat pattern of correspondence between the old testament and the new, and to speak of the old testament preparing for or foreshadowing the new is perhaps the most eloquent tribute to the interpretative acumen of their forebears.

The author of Hebrews is a past master in this kind of interpretation: the reading of the old testament in the light of Christ. In their original setting the passages which he assembles in 1:5–14 refer either to God himself or to the Jewish king or messiah, but he applies them to Christ, thus expressing his faith in Christ's transcendent sonship and divinity. It is possible that some of these passages, particularly Ps 2 and Ps 110, figured in a chain of selected old testament texts which the author is using as one of his sources. In comparing the Son with the angels he also puts these latter in their right place. They are inferior not only to the Son and heir but also to men who, in Christ, are sons and heirs, since angels are at the service of the covenant which is for the benefit of men (1:7, 14).

(b) Heb 2:1–4. Exhortation to take God's word seriously

The angels administered to men (1:14) especially, according to Jewish tradition, as mediators of the old law (cf Gal 3:19). As great as was the attention which this required, God's word, addressed to us in Christ, demands even more

intense concentration and is likewise accompanied by
more serious threats. The author states clearly that the
definiteness and finality of God's saving revelation (1:14;
2:3) demands a corresponding resolute, complete, un-
reserved and irreversible commitment of faith on man's
part. He will return frequently to this fundamental idea.
2:3b–4 refers to Jesus' own preaching of the gospel, to its
attestation by the first apostles (cf 13:7; Luke 24:48; Acts
1:8) and to the various *charismata* bestowed on the church
by the Holy Spirit (cf 1 Cor 12; Rom 12:3–8; Eph 4:7–
12).

(c) Heb 2:5–9. The man Jesus and the angels

Having shown that the Son is superior to the angels as
'God' (1:5–13) and intimated that the angels, as servants,
are inferior to men (1:14), the author now demonstrates
that Jesus (named for the first time in 2:9) is superior to
the angels even as man. He does this by a clever application of Ps 8 to Christ, with special stress on the idea of
subjection (2:5, 8). In its original setting Ps 8:4–6 concerns man's place within creation (cf Gen 1:26f). It is
not certain that the Jews at the time of Christ understood
it as a reference to the future messiah, but it does bear
striking similarities with the ideas of Ps 110:1, which the
author has already quoted (1:13; cf 1:3) and which was
more probably such a messianic psalm. Certainly it is well
worth noting the close link between Ps 110 and Ps 8 in the
author's mind. Here he understands Ps 8 as a prophecy of
the *eschaton*, the end of God's plan for man. The world
which is subject to man (cf Ps 8:6) is not this world, that
is, not the universe as we now experience it, but the world
to come (cf 6:5), that is, the world into which God has
introduced his Son by the resurrection (cf 1:6). Thus the

'man' of Ps 8 is not, in the author's mind, mankind in general but the man Jesus (2:9) who, by the incarnation (cf 2:14; 5:7), was for a little while lower than the angels (2:7, 9) but, by the resurrection, was crowned with glory and honour (ibid). To suit his purpose, the author even changes the original 'little less than the gods' (Ps 8:5) to 'for a little while lower than the angels' (2:7). His thought is very close to that of the magnificent christological hymn in Phil 2:5–11, according to which Jesus achieves his glory through the humiliation of the cross, only in the present passage the idea of the solidarity of all men (2:9) with Christ is emphasised. Jesus is indeed *the man* of Ps 8, the only one who has achieved the human fulfilment assigned to man in Ps 8, but he has done so as *Man*, the first-born (cf 12:23; 1:6) of a new humanity (cf Col 1:15) which corresponds exactly to God's original design. Jesus by his passion, death and resurrection has become the *real* man of Ps 8, the authentic Adam of Gen 1–2 (cf 1 Cor 15:20–28, 42–50; Rom 5:14). From now on, man, God's image (Gen 1:26; Wis 1:23), will achieve his fulfilment, live up to his vocation, only in so far as he is modelled on Jesus, *Man*, the image of God (cf 1:3; cf Col 1:15).

It is probable that the identification of Jesus with the man of Ps 8 was facilitated by reflexion on the phrase 'son of man' in Ps 8:4, since this was Jesus' favourite self-designation (cf Mt 16:13f). It is interesting to observe that Jesus, at his trial before the sanhedrin, also connects the title 'Son of Man' with Ps 110 (Mt 26:54 par). The reference to Dan 7:14 is here explicit and the Son of Man in Daniel seems to be both an individual and an incorporation of the whole of God's people. Thus this title was particularly felicitous as a preparation for the important theme of the incorporation of all men in Christ (cf Col 1:18–20). It is also most striking that the Son of Man in

Daniel triumphs through the suffering of persecution, which is precisely the tenor of Mt 26:54 par and Heb 2:5–9.

In explicitly referring to Jesus' sufferings and death as 'the grace of God' (2:9), the author suggests both that the fulfilment achieved by Jesus for everyone is a pure gift and that the redemption (cf 9:15) and the shedding of blood (cf 9:14) which it involved were not the paying a price nor the appeasing the wrath of an angry God but were themselves a gift of God. Jesus' death was a gift, a *charis*, which he acknowledged in his *eucharist* (cf Mt 26:26 par).

(d) Heb 2:10–18. Incarnation and priesthood

The author now explains the main ideas of the previous section: God's initiative, Christ's primacy and the solidarity of all men with Christ. The *raison d'être* of the Christ-event is that God should bring many sons to glory through Christ, the pioneer of salvation (2:10; cf 13:20). Christ's glory is to be shared by all men who will thus become sons in the Son. This solidarity with Christ has a real or ontological character; it is based on the Son's sharing in human nature (2:11–18, cf 4:15), but it also has what might be called an exemplary or moral character, that is, it necessarily involves man's response to Jesus' example. As the new Adam, Christ incorporates the whole of humanity, but this 'newness' becomes a reality for men only in so far as they follow their pioneer which, in practical terms, means grasping the nettle of suffering and eventual death in Christ's spirit and following his example (cf I Pet 2:21). Jesus experienced death for everyone not 'from without', as one man substituting for all, but 'from within' as the man who incorporates all who must, in their turn, ratify in their own lives what Christ has established by his paschal mystery (cf Rom 8:17). This relationship between the ontological and exemplary aspects of the Christ-event is central in the author's thought and is the basis of his remarkable oscillation between doctrinal exposition and moral exhortation. Throughout the whole work, Jesus is presented as *the* exemplar for men, and the Christ-event as *the* structure of fulfilled human existence. But Jesus is not merely a good example of what men should be. The incarnation means that God has effected a real and radical change in the human situation. In Christ humanity has achieved its fulfilment.

The realism of the incarnation is a consequence of *man's* need for salvation (cf 1:14; 2:3, 10). The Son became man because it was man and not angels who needed redemption (2:16). The Son neither is an angel (1:5–14) nor did he become one.

The passage of Jesus, the Man, from suffering and death to glory (cf 2:9) means that death, the ultimate scandal for the human mind, man's last enemy (cf 1 Cor 15:26, 54–55) has been defeated. Man is thus liberated from his most profound fear, and the devil who, according to Jewish tradition (cf Wis 2:24) had the power of death, has been destroyed (2:14–15).

To prove the reality of the incarnation from the old testament the author applies to Christ Ps 22:22 and Is 8:17–18 (2:12–13) exploiting the words 'brethren' (cf 2:17) and 'children' (cf 2:14). He also re-introduces (cf 1:3) what will become a major theme of his work: the priesthood of Christ (2:11 and 17). Hebrews is the only new testament writing which gives the title 'high priest' or 'priest' to Christ and which describes the Christ-event explicitly in priestly terms. Whatever the source of the author's thoughts, he alone has had the ingenuity to develop this motif. Here he relates it to the incarnation. The Christ-event has created a profound change of relationship between humanity and God, a sharing in God's glory (cf 2:10). This could be expressed in terms of sanctification or consecration (cf Jn 17:17-19), of which the high priest, according to judaism, was the principal mediator (cf Lev 16). The high priest was 'he who sanctifies', the people 'those who are sanctified' (2:11). But just as the consecration or sanctification involved in the Christ-event (cf 10:10) is not merely ritual but real, so Christ's priesthood is real. He *is* God's holy, consecrated one (cf Jn 6:69; 10:36) who, by the self-consecration of his passion, death and resurrection, effects the real conversion of men from sin to holiness (cf Heb 13:12; Jn 17:17-19). Clearly the term 'consecration' as the allied cultic words: 'high priest', 'priest', 'expiation', 'sacrifice' and 'offering', when applied to the unique and transcendent Christ-event, are images or symbols but they do express an underlying unity of meaning between the old testament cult and what God has done in Christ. In Christ mankind has *really* entered into a relationship which was only *symbolically* (cf 9:9) represented in the old testament. The author is addressing people steeped in Jewish ritual and its symbolism and he finds in these a useful means for communicating his message. He presents the incarnation as a kind of ordination ceremony to the high priesthood (2:17) which Jesus will exercise in three successive stages: throughout his life (5:7), at his passion, death and resurrection (9:11-14) and now at his continued exaltation (cf 6:20; 7:25; 9:24). A partaker in human nature (2:14), Jesus also shares the human condition and so is a source of comfort and encouragement (2:18; cf 4:15). He helps 'those who are tempted', that is, those who suffer the trials of human existence, in so far as he is their pioneer (2:10; cf 6:20; 12:2) and leads the way from suffering to glory (cf Jn 14:6). It is not so much that Jesus is a man like us, but that he is the Son who became man with the specific purpose of leading us to the Father (cf Jn 20:17). The high-priestly image applied to Christ is a cultic variant of the thought expressed in 2:5–9. Jesus, as our high priest, represents us to God not simply as one among many, but as the one incorporating the many. It is interesting to note, in this regard, that in some areas of judaism Adam was often presented as the high priest of humanity.

1. Why does the author introduce the theme of angels here?

2. Compare the revelation of God in the old testament to the revelation in the new.

3. Discuss the radical response demanded by the christian commitment.

4. Analyse the author's use of Ps 8. What use is exegesis of the old testament for us today?

5. How does the author understand the purpose of the incarnation?

3

Exhortation to faithfulness and confidence Heb 3:1–5:10

(a) Heb 3:1–6. Jesus and Moses

After the doctrinal section (2:5–18) comes the moral exhortation. As important as the teaching on Christ's priesthood is, it is used by the author as a basis for what he considers to be even more important: the christian's life of faith, faithfulness, hope, confidence and persever-ance. These virtues are stressed repeatedly throughout the letter and are the main object of the author's endeavour (cf 13:22).

The dynamic character of the Christ-event, whereby the Son becomes man and passes through death to glory (cf 2:8–9, 10) moulds the nature of the whole of christian existence. Man is destined for glory beyond the present structures of this world. Because the Son has shared his nature (cf 2:14), man now shares in the Son's heavenly exaltation (3:1). Only this exaltation is through suffering (cf Lk 24:26; Phil 2:5–11). Hence the necessity of fixing our attention on the 'pioneer' of our salvation (cf 2:10) who was sent (3:1) especially to show us precisely how to live, suffer and die. The Jewish high-priest had the privilege of entering into the holy of holies, the repre-sentation of God's dwelling place (cf 8:5; 9:3, 7, 24),

once a year (cf 9:7). But Jesus our high priest has entered
into heaven itself (cf 4:14; 6:19; 9:24), the real holy of
holies (cf 9:12) and this once for all (ibid). Following him
there involves living, suffering and, ultimately, dying as
he did. For the christian the whole of life is a liturgy,
more precisely, a procession through this world into the
holy of holies of heaven in the train of Jesus the high
priest. Yet this pilgrimage through the world is neither
an attempted escape from it nor a stiff upper-lip stoic
attitude to adversity. It is the firm grasping of the realities
of human existence in the spirit of Jesus, our 'pioneer'
(cf 12:1–2).

In 1:5–2:18 the author has shown that Jesus is far
superior to the angels. Now (3:2–6) he shows that he is
superior in faithfulness (cf 2:17) to Moses, the mediator
of the old covenant. The source of this superiority is again
Jesus' divine Sonship (3:6; cf 1:2, 5, 8).

(b) Heb 3:7–4:11. Exhortation to faithfulness

Belonging to God's house (cf 3:6), sharing in the Son's
glory (cf 2:10), is a dynamic not a static reality. It depends
upon the response of persevering faith, faithfulness, confidence and hope (3:6, 14), The author, therefore, exhorts
his readers to these virtues and having already evoked the
figure of Moses (cf 3:2–6), draws the parallel between the
events of the exodus, under Moses' leadership (3:16) and
the christian's situation in the desert of this world
(cf 1 Cor 10:1–13).

The whole of life for the christian is a continuous
exodus, attended by various trials of which those of the
historical exodus were only types or symbols. God's house
(cf 3:6), the church (cf 12:23), is the new people of God
(4:9) *en route* for the promised land of heaven and beset

with all manner of difficulties on the way. It will arrive at its destination, the promised rest (3:11, 18; 4:1, 3, 5, 9, 10, 11) only in, with and through Jesus, the new and superior Joshua (4:8), in so far as it imitates his faithfulness (cf 2:17; 3:2).

(c) Heb 4:12–13. The incisiveness of God's word

The author has already contrasted the gospel to the old law (cf 2:1–4). He now underlines its superior effectiveness. Even in the old testament man was judged by his attitude to the law, God's word. But with the definiteness and decisiveness of God's revelation in the new (cf 1:2), man's own attitude has become more crucial and critical. God has now spoken clearly and distinctly in his Son made man. Nothing is more familiar, more accessible, more knowable to man than human nature and this is where God has finally communicated with him. Just as God has ultimately approached man in Christ, so man encounters God most decisively in him. Man's attitude to God's word in Christ is his own judge (cf Jn 3:18; 5:24; 12:47–48). Man cannot, therefore, remain indifferent to Christ. Christ brings man into judgement.

(d) Heb 4:15–5:10. Exhortation to confidence

The very stringent demands made on the christian by the supreme example of Christ's own faithfulness (cf 3:2–6) and the inexorable scrutiny of God's word (cf 4:12–13), combined with the author's threatening tone in 3:7–4:11, could produce a depressing effect were they not balanced by a consideration of Jesus' compassion and mercy (cf 2:17–18). In the present section, therefore, the author applies himself to this latter. Whereas in 3:1–6 Jesus was presented as an example of faithfulness, now he is held out as a source of confidence and encouragement (4:14–16).

In 5:1–10 the author compares and contrasts Jesus, the high priest, to the Jewish high priest. The latter is taken from among men (5:1), whereas Jesus, the Son of God (cf 4:14) became man in order to be a high priest (cf 2:17), was sent (cf 3:1) to be a high priest. This is the most profound difference between Jesus' priesthood and that of judaism or of any other religion. Jesus' priesthood involved not his being separated from men but his being sent to them, becoming one of them (cf 2:17). His is an apostolic priesthood. And this mission of the Son to men was necessary if the cycle of human sinfulness was to be broken. For although appointed to 'offer gifts and sacrifices for sins' (5:1; cf 2:17), the purely human priest had still 'to offer sacrifice for his own sins' (5:3). His weakness (5:2) extended to sinfulness, whereas Jesus was sinless (cf 4:15; Jn 8:46; 2 Cor 5:21). Only the sinless one is able to make effective expiation for sin.

Both the Jewish high priest and Christ are called by God but the former is 'taken from among men' (5:1) as Aaron was (5:4), whereas Jesus' priesthood is identified with his Sonship (5:5). Ps 2:7 (cf 1:5) originally referred most probably to the adoption of a Jewish king as son of God (cf 2 Sam 7:14). It later became a prophecy of the future messiah. Early christian tradition applied it to Jesus' resurrection which was thus considered to be a heavenly enthronement ceremony (Ac 13:33; Rom 1:4). The author here likewise applies it to the resurrection envisaged as an ordination ceremony (5:9; cf 2:17), but he also seems to have in mind the eternal generation of the Son by the Father (5:8; cf 1:2, 5, 5; 3:6; 4:14). There is no contradiction between these two ideas of Jesus' eternal sonship and his messianic sonship. The early christians first understood that this man Jesus had become 'Lord and Christ' (cf Ac 2:36), the son of God in the messianic sense, by the resurrection (cf Rom 1:4). But gradually they realised that Jesus had only become by the resurrection what he had always been by nature, namely, God's Son in the fullest sense of the term. Ps 2:7, interpreted as a reference to Jesus' messianic enthronement, naturally attracts Ps 110 (5:6), another royal psalm with a similar history to that of Ps 2 (cf 1:3, 13). Ps 110 is the most quoted old testament passage in the whole of the new testament and has possibly been more influential than any other. It certainly plays a vital role in Hebrews. Its first verse is frequently applied to Christ's resurrection, as is Ps 2:7 (cf Ac 2:33–35; 5:31). Here, however, the author exploits Ps 110:4, which contains an explicit reference to the king's or messiah's priesthood (cf 1:3). Applied to Christ, this means that by his resurrection he has become 'a priest forever' (5:10). This verse and especially the phrase 'forever', will exercise a major influence in the author's ensuing arguments. For the present, it serves to demonstrate that Jesus' priesthood is royal rather than Aaronic (5:4; cf 7:11) or levitical (cf 7:4–14).

In the author's mind offering is an integral part of priesthood (5:1, 3; cf 8:3). Christ's earthly priesthood, however, did not consist in the offering of gifts and sacrifices (5:1, 3; cf 8:3) but in prayers and supplications (5:7), and his salvation from death, or his resurrection, was the fruit of his 'godly fear'. There is a possible reference here to Jesus' prayer in the garden (cf Mt 26:36f par), but more important is the spiritualisation of 'offering' and, therefore, of priesthood in terms of prayer (cf 6:20; 7:25, Rom 8:34).

By way of a résumé, 5:8–10 describe the whole structure of the Christ-event from the pre-existence of the Son

(5:8) to his designation as 'high priest' at the resurrection (5:10). Both the objective and the subjective aspects of salvation (5:9; cf 1:14; 2:3, 10) are emphasized. Christ is the source of salvation (5:9) but only to those who obey him with an obedience modelled upon his own, learnt through suffering (5:8; cf 12:5–11). The further allusion to Ps 110:4 prepares for the author's later developments (cf 6:20f).

1. Why does the author compare Jesus with Moses?

2. Is the theme of the exodus meaningful for us today?

3. What does the author mean by 'the word of God', and why does he compare it with a sword?

4. How does the author understand Jesus as the basis of our confidence?

4

Subject and purpose of the letter
Heb 5:11–6:20

(a) Heb 5:11–14. Reprimand for immaturity

The author here pauses to inform his readers that the doctrine of Christ's eternal priesthood and the response which it requires is strong meat and not digestible by those who appear to have neglected their christian education. A key-word here is 'mature' (5:14), which is only a variant of the fulfilment or perfection achieved by Christ (cf 2:10; 5:9).

(b) Heb 6:1–8. Exhortation to maturity

Having reprimanded his readers for their lack of maturity, the author now invites them to take their education more seriously and to strive for maturity (6:1). 6:1–2 give us an interesting compendium of the catechism of the early church and what the author styles 'the first principles' (cf 5:12) or the 'foundation' (6:1) of christian teaching. In 6:3 the author announces his intention to return to the more mature teaching of Christ's priesthood (cf 5:11). In 6:4–8 on the impossibility of a second repentance (cf 10:26–31; 12:17) he does not deny the possibility of all repentance for sin (cf 12:12–13). The repentance in question is that of 6:1, that is, the fundamental act of

27

conversion which is at the origin of the whole of the christian life. There can be only one such conversion. All other repentance involves not going back to the beginning again, but progressing on to the end, to maturity or fulfilment. The apostasy concerned (6:6; cf 3:12) is the deliberate renunciation of the Son of God. The author's thought must be seen against the background of his view on the clarity, definitiveness and absoluteness of God's revelation in Christ (cf 1 : 1; 2 : 2–4; 4 : 12–13). God has spoken so trenchantly in his Son that once this has been recognised, accepted and rejected it is impossible to accept again—precisely because there will never be any more convincing indications than those already given. The impossibility of repentance (6:4) is thus more a psychological impotence in the apostate than an inability or unwillingness in God to forgive.

(c) Heb 6:9–20. Encouragement and exhortation to hope

As in 4 : 14–16, the author modifies what may appear as a very sombre view of the christian life (6 : 4–8; cf 4 : 12–13) with his predominant motif of encouragement and exhortation (cf 13 : 22). His readers clearly do not belong to the category mentioned in 6 : 4–8 (6 : 9) but, as the author sees it, the christian life involves progress, continuous movement to the end (6 : 11). Instead, therefore, of merely commending them for their work and love (6 : 10), he urges them on to the 'full assurance of hope' (6 : 11), following the example of their ancestors, in faith, patience and hope (6 : 12–18; cf 11 : 1–40; 13 : 7).

6 : 13–18 contains a characteristic piece of the author's rabbinical exegesis. By concentrating on the ideas of swearing and oath, found in Gen 22 : 10, he intends to

demonstrate that christians have a double source of consolation and encouragement (6:18): God's promise and
God's oath. The 'fleeing for refuge' (6:18) might indicate
an escape from a physical or moral danger, say, from the
destruction of a city (cf 11:10, 16; 13:14) or the persecution or attraction of judaism (cf 13:13). But, since the
author here associates himself with his readers, it is more
likely to be an imaginative description of christians who,
by vocation (cf 3:1), are on the run towards the heavenly
Jerusalem (cf 12:22; 13:13–14), their only sure resting-
place (cf 4:9). Christians, however, have even more than
God's promise and oath as a basis for their hope, since
that hope itself has been realised in the person of Jesus
(6:19–20; cf 12:2). The actual presence of Jesus, the
Man, in the holy of holies of heaven (cf 4:14) is the surest
guarantee of the seriousness of God's word. In Jesus the
end (6:11) has already been achieved. Moreover, he is not
only our forerunner, the first fruits (1 Cor 15:20). He has
gone behind the curtain (6:19; cf 9:3) as a high priest
'on our behalf', that is, to exercise his eternal priesthood
of intercession (6:20; cf 7:25; 9:24; Rom 8:34). As in
5:7, the author identifies Jesus' priestly activity with
prayer, only here it is a question of heavenly intercession
from after the resurrection, with the emphasis on the
'forever' of Ps 110:4.

*1. How would the author's reprimand for immaturity
apply to us today?*

*2. What has Hebrews to say about repentance, and how
is this related to the sacrament of penance?*

5

Excellence of Jesus' priesthood
Heb 7:1–28

(a) Heb 7:–10. Melchizedek and Abraham

The previous section (6 : 9–20) contained an implicit contrast between the double basis of Abraham's patience and hope: God's promise and oath and that of christians: the heavenly priesthood of Christ. The author now explicitly contrasts Melchizedek as a type of Christ (7 : 3), to Abraham in order to extol the superiority of the former over the latter, as he has already done with regard to both Moses (cf 3 : 1–6) and Joshua (cf 4 : 8).

After evoking the scene recorded in Gen 14 : 17–20 (9 : 1–2) he first wishes to prove that, both in virtue of his name and the lack of any mention of ancestry in Gen 14, Melchizedek is a figure or type of Jesus the Son of God (7 : 3; cf 1 : 2, 5, 6; 3 : 6; 4 : 14; 5 : 5, 8). Clearly there is no question here of Gen 14 containing, however implicitly, the revelation of Jesus' sonship. Rather, the author, as a rabbinical exegete, exploits this passage in favour of his faith in this revelation.

Melchizedek's superiority over Abraham is further emphasised, in the author's mind, by the fact that Melchizedek both blessed Abraham and received tithes from him (7 : 4–10). And since Abraham 'contained' the levitical priesthood (7 : 10) this latter was by that very fact inferior to Melchizedek's. 7 : 8 again attracts attention to the eternal or 'living' character of Melchizedek's priest-hood (cf 5 : 6; 6 : 20; 7 : 3), fulfilled in Christ (cf 7 : 16) as opposed to the mortal character of the levitical priesthood.

(b) 7:11–28. Melchizedek's priesthood and the levitical priesthood

The old testament's prophecy of a new order of priest-hood is an eloquent witness to the fact that the levitical priesthood, as well as the law of which it was only a part, was unable to bring the people to fulfilment. The change in priesthood necessarily involves a change in the law (7 : 11–12). This prophecy has been accomplished in the person of Jesus, who did not belong to the tribe of Levi which alone had the prerogative of the priesthood, but to Judah, the royal tribe and, therefore, the tribe of the royal priesthood, according to the order of Melchizedek (7 : 13–14). The faith in the resurrection of Jesus clinches the whole argument. Jesus' passage from death to life is his ordination to a living (7 : 8) and eternal priesthood. His enthronement as the messiah (Ps 110: cf 1 : 1, 13; 5 : 5) carries with it his investiture as the messianic high priest (17 : 15–17; cf 5 : 6, 8; 6 : 20; 7 : 11, 18). All this entails that the old law (7 : 11–12) has been abrogated because of its impotence and a new way of access to God has been intro-duced (7 : 18–19; cf 6 : 19–20).

As in his exegesis of Gen 22 : 16–17 (cf 6 : 13–18), the author here emphasises the idea of oath in Ps 110 : 4 in order to prove still further the superiority of the christian dispensation (7 : 20–22). He also introduces the notion of covenant (7 : 22) which he will develop later (cf 8 : 6f).

As the author has suggested in 5 : 3, the only high priest capable of effectively saving from sin is one who is both sinless (cf 4 : 16) and has actually entered the holy of

holies of heaven (cf 4:14), since only he is exempt from
the need to offer sacrifices for his own sins before acting
on behalf of the people. Jesus' sacrifice (cf 5:1) consisted
in the once for all offering of himself by which he entered
the divine presence in his human nature (7:26–27). The
author thus sees a sixfold contrast between Jesus and the
levitical priests (7:23–24). Jesus is one, they are many.
His ministry is eternal, theirs is temporary (7:23–25). He
is holy, they are sinful (7:26–27). His ministry is
heavenly, theirs is earthly (7:26; cf 8:4f). His sacrifice is
unique, theirs is multiple (7:27). His sacrifice is of himself, theirs is of victims other than themselves (7:27).
But the basis of all these contrasts is the fact that the
levitical high priests are only men (cf 5:1), whereas Jesus
is the Son of God become man (7:28; cf 4:14). The only
high priest capable of saving man is one who is not taken
from men (cf 5:1) but sent to them (cf 3:1).

1. Discuss the author's exegesis of Gen 14 and Ps 110.

*2. What is the relation between the law and the priest-
hood?*

*3. How are we to understand the abrogation of the
levitical priesthood and its supersession by Christ?*

6

Excellence of Christ's high priestly liturgy and mediation Heb 8:1–10:18

(a) Heb 8:1–5. Heavenly priesthood and sanctuary

In 7:26 the author has stipulated what kind of high priest the logic of God's plan requires. He now stresses that in fact we have such a high priest in Christ and places special emphasis on the heavenly character of his ministry (cf 7:26). To understand the author's thought here it is vital to grasp that he does not mean 'heaven' or 'heavenly' in a topographical sense but in a qualitative sense. He does not wish to say that Christ is now actually exercising a liturgy in the heavenly sanctuary. His insistence on the once for all character of Christ's sacrifice (cf 7:27; 9:12, 26, 28; 10:10, 12, 13) is sufficient proof of this. By the 'heavenly' imagery he wishes to bring out the superior quality of Christ's liturgy vis-à-vis the 'earthly' liturgy of judaism (cf 11:16). What he contrasts to this latter is not Christ's continuous priestly ministry 'in heaven' but his unique self-offering, his paschal mystery, consisting of his passion, death and resurrection. As in the case of priesthood (cf 2:11, 17), we are here presented with a projection into the heavenly, superior or transcendent order of an idea which the author has derived from his experience of the actual Jewish liturgy. He is trying to make the

33

unique, transcendent Christ-event meaningful to readers who are imbued with, fascinated and almost seduced by (cf 13:9–14) this liturgy with all its splendour. Although he stresses that Christ's paschal mystery is not liturgy as it was experienced by the Jews (8:2, 4), he nevertheless emphasises that it is liturgy in that it corresponds to what the Jewish liturgy really stood for, or represented (cf 7:26). It is the true liturgy of which the Jewish liturgy was but a 'copy and shadow' (8:2, 4; cf 9:24). The heavenly character of Christ's liturgy is supported by the fact that as far as the earth was concerned, that is, judaism, he was a layman, not belonging to the tribe of Levi but to the tribe of Judah (8:4; cf 7:13–14). His liturgy is not of this world (8:2; cf 9:11, 24). But it is a liturgy. It must, therefore, be other than this world, that is 'heavenly', as opposed to 'earthly'.

(b) Heb 8:6–13. Mediator of the new covenant

The author has announced the motif of a better covenant in 7:22. He now uses it to prove the excellence of Christ's ministry. Covenant involves liturgy so that the change in the one brings about a change in the other (8:7). His argument is very similar to that in 7:11–12; 18–19. There, however, it was a change in the priesthood which entailed a change in the law, whereas here it is a change of the covenant which has effected a change in the liturgy. In both cases the author is at pains to show that the old testament itself spotted the radical inadequacy of its own institutions and pointed towards better ones (8:7, 13; cf 7:11, 18). Jer 31:31–34 is the longest old testament passage quoted in the new testament. It serves the author's purpose admirably to establish both the promise of Christ's new liturgy (8:6, 13; cf 9:15–22) and the final forgiveness of sins (8:12; cf 10:17–18).

(c) Heb 9:1–10. The liturgy of the old covenant

The author's aim is clearly to draw a parallel between the Christ-event and the Jewish liturgy. He therefore first describes the apparatus (9:1–5) and the procedure (9:6–10) which the latter involves, concentrating his attention on the liturgy of the *Yom Kippur*, the great day of expiations (cf Lev 16; cf 2:17; 8:12). This was *the* great liturgy of the Jewish high priest in which, once a year, he alone entered the holy of holies (9:7) to make expiation for the sins of the people. It is interesting to observe that the liturgy which is described, albeit very schematically (9:5), is not that of the Jerusalem temple but that of the tabernacle in the desert (cf 3:7–4:11). True to his method (cf 7:11–12; 8:7, 13) the author interprets the respective duties of the priest and high priest symbolically, as a witness to the inaccessibility of the true sanctuary (9:8; cf 8:2) as long as the 'outer tent' (9:8) is still standing. The 'sanctuary' here stands for the holy of holies of heaven (cf 4:14; 9:12) and the 'outer tent' stands for the whole complex of the Jewish liturgy. It is implied that Christ's paschal mystery marks the end of the whole of the Jewish liturgy: temple, sacrifice, priesthood and all that they involved. Jewish law and liturgy have become obsolete (cf 7:12, 18; 8:7, 13) more, have been abolished in Christ, and to remain attached to them is to support an obstacle to true access to God (cf 13:9–14). All this was symbolised by the rending of the temple curtain at Christ's death (cf 6:13; Mt 27:51 par). The author is reluctant to admit that the Jewish high priest offers for the sins of the people (9:7; cf 2:17; 5:1, 3; 7:27) because, in view of the Christ-event, the 'gifts and sacrifices' offered (9:9–10; cf 5:1, 3; 7:27) have a merely external efficacy.

(d) Heb 9:11–14. Christ's liturgy

The author now opposes Christ's passion, death and resurrection to the Jewish liturgy according to a threefold structure of continuation, rupture and transcendence. He shows that Christ, by his paschal mystery, is a high priest, and does perform a liturgy; that this priesthood and liturgy are not those of the old testament; and that they transcend or excel those of the old testament. This excellence consists in the fact that Christ has entered heaven itself, as opposed to the earthly holy of holies (9:11–12; cf 1:3; 4:14; 8:1–2; 9:24; 12:2); that this has taken place once for all, as opposed to the multiplicity of the old testament ministry (9:12; cf 7:27; 9:26, 28; 10:10) and even to the yearly offering of the Jewish high priest (cf 9:7, 25); that it was accomplished not by the offering of dead animals and the sprinkling of their blood, but by the self-offering of Christ and the sprinkling of his own blood (9:12; cf 7:27; 9:19, 27, 28; 10:10); and, finally, that the effect of this liturgy is an eternal and spiritual redemption as opposed to the temporal and carnal redemption of the old testament rites (9:12–14; cf 9:9–10). The whole aim of this 'redemption' (9:12) is to introduce the christian into the worship of the living God. Christ's priesthood has as its supreme effect the priesthood of the faithful (9:14; cf 12:28; 13:15–16).

(e) Heb 9:15–24. Christ's mediation

The author now returns to the theme of the covenant, left in 9:1, and illustrates Christ's excellence not only as the 'high priest' of the *Yom Kippur* (cf 9:1–14), but also as the mediator of the new covenant (cf 8:6f) of whom Moses (9:19; cf 3:2–6) was the type. By a characteristic play on the Greek term for covenant—*diatheke*—which can be translated by both 'covenant' and 'will', he shows how Christ's death fulfils the requirements of the new covenant. This death has the double effect of giving access to our inheritance (cf 1:4, 14; 12:17) and of redeeming us (cf 9:12) from the transgressions under the first covenant (9:15–16). The imagery of 'redemption' (9:12, 15) emphasises the fact that by Christ's death men have been delivered from the slavery of sin (cf 2:14–15) and given to the service of the living God (cf 9:14). The imagery of inheritance highlights the fact that in Christ's death and resurrection men have become sons in the Son (cf 2:10; Rom 8:14–17). Christ's blood, previously identified with the blood of expiation (9:12–14), is now seen to be the blood of the covenant (9:17–20; cf Mt 26:28 par) and his death, therefore, the sacrifice of the new covenant (cf Ex 24:4–8), which creates God's new people. Similarly, the sprinkling of Christ's blood is regarded as the purifying of the heavenly sanctuary (9:21–23). This does not imply that the author considers the heavens (cf 8:1) to be 'impure' in any way. He is rather trying to express the transcendent reality of Christ's paschal mystery in the different images suggested to him by the Jewish liturgy and, having already established a parallel between 'the heavens' and the earthly sanctuary (cf 8:1f), he now brings in the idea of a purifying ceremony to complete the picture. In 9:24 he resumes the whole movement of his thought since 8:1. The resurrection of Christ is clearly more than a return to the life of this world with its present structures. It is his entry into a new dimension of existence (cf 2:9), what is meaningfully symbolised for a Jew by entry 'into heaven' (cf 4:14). In Jewish thought the temple or sanctuary was taken to be a replica of heaven, God's real home. By his entry in heaven, therefore, Jesus has, in cultic terms, entered the true sanctuary, where he is present as our high priest, on our behalf (9:24; cf 6:20; 7:25). Once again the author envisages Christ's heavenly exaltation as itself an aspect of his high priestly activity of intercession (cf 5:7).

(f) 9:25-28. Christ's unique and definitive self-sacrifice and his second coming

In order to avoid a purely materialistic interpretation of Christ's presence in the 'heavenly sanctuary' (cf 9:24) the author again stresses the once-for-all character of Christ's sacrifice (cf 7:27). There is no question of Christ offering a repeated sacrifice, since his sacrifice is unique: his self-offering in his death (9:25-26; cf 9:14). Since man can die only once (9:27), it follows that the death of the Son in his human nature (cf 2:9) marks the end of the world (9:26; cf 1:2), which has nothing more to expect but Christ's second appearance to those 'who are eagerly waiting for him' (9:28). Christian existence is doubly eschatological: on the one hand, it moves towards the end (cf 6:11); on the other, it already enjoys the end (cf 9:26) and waits for its final manifestation at Christ's second coming.

(g) Heb 10:1-4. Inefficacy of the law's sacrifices

Here the author virtually repeats what he has already said in 9:9-10. The continued repetition of the old testament sacrifices is itself a witness to their impotence to abolish sins, simply because they are mere exterior rites.

(h) Heb 10:5-10. Efficacy of Christ's sacrifice

On the contrary, Christ's sacrifice was efficacious because it consisted of the union of his will with God's in fulfilment of Ps 40:6–8. It was not the mere shedding of Christ's blood which made his death a sacrifice but the filial love which it expressed (cf 5:7), the Spirit in which it was performed (cf 9:14).

(i) Heb 10:11–18. Efficacy of Christ's priesthood and mediation

Similarly, the Jewish priests' repeated ministry is a sign of their radical inadequacy and inability to abolish sins (cf 9:25). Christ, on the contrary, offered but one sacrifice (10:12) and afterwards 'sat down' at God's right hand (cf 1:3) and is now waiting (cf 9:28) for the final manifestation of his victory over sin. The uniqueness of Christ's offering is proved by the fact that the new covenant, of which he is the mediator (cf 8:6; 9:15), involves the definitive forgiveness of sins. There is no sacrifice for sins other than Christ's self-offering (10:18). The definitiveness of God's revelation in his Son (cf 1:2) is matched by the definitiveness of the Son's sacrifice (cf 10:14), which means that there is no salvation outside Christ (cf 6:4–8; 10:26–31; 12:17; Ac 4:12).

1. *What does Hebrews mean by 'heaven' and 'heavenly'?*

2. *Discuss the importance of Jer 31:31–34.*

3. *How does Hebrews consider the relation between the Christ-event and the liturgy of judaism?*

4. *How is Christ the mediator of the new covenant?*

5. *What relevance has the author's understanding of Christ's unique sacrifice to our conception of the eucharist and the ministry?*

6. *How is Christ's second appearance related to the first?*

7. Why were the sacrifices of the old testament ineffective?

8. Why was Christ's sacrifice effective?

7

Exhortation to faithfulness and other virtues Heb 10:19–12:28

(a) Heb 10:19–31. Exhortation to sincerity, faithfulness and love

The doctrine of Christ's priesthood and liturgy which the author has been elaborating since 7:1 as a basis of consolation and encouragement (cf 6:9–20), is again presented explicitly as the motive of confidence (10:19–21). The christian has access to God, that is he worships him (cf 9:14), and shares in Christ's liturgy, by sincerity and faith as opposed to the external ritual of the old testament (cf 9:9–10; 13:16). It is these virtues which are the true purification of the conscience, the real washing of the body (10:22). It is possible that the latter phrase refers to baptism (cf 6:4). In 10:23 the author renews his exhortation to faithfulness and perseverance (cf 3:1–4:14; 6:9–12). The third exhortation (cf 10:22, 23) concerns the christian's communal life of 'love and good works' (10:24; cf 6:10; 13:1–16), meeting together and mutual encouragement (10:25). Progress in the christian life depends on active membership of the community. At the end of 10:25 the author again evokes the expectation of Christ's final manifestation (cf 9:28; 10:14).

After the positive motive for progressing in the christian life comes the negative threat of judgement (10:26–31). The clear implication is that there is no standing still in the christian life. One is either going forward (10:19–25) or falling backwards (10:26–31). The author does not think in terms of shades but simply of black and white (cf 2:1–4; 6:4–8). His strong language suggests that the sin involved (10:26) is the radical apostasy of 6:4–8 (cf 3:12), but the definiteness of God's revelation in Christ is such that the refusal to respond to it is already such apostasy. As with God's word (cf 4:12–13), it is impossible to remain indifferent to the Son of God, the blood of the covenant and the Spirit of grace (10:29) revealed in Christ. Not to persevere *is* to sin (cf 12:1).

(b) Heb 10:32–39. Encouragement and exhortation to confidence and perseverance

In 10:31, the author ended on a somewhat fearful note. Now, as in 4:14–5:10 and 6:9–20, he proffers a word of encouragement, reminding his readers of their past virtues (10:32–34, cf 6:9–11). He sees even in these, however, a further motive for their perseverance. Are they going to give up now, having been so courageous in the past, especially when the end is so near (10:37–39; cf 10:25)? The quotation from Hab 2:3–4 serves admirably to express the author's thought on the imminence of the end, the necessity of faith and its dynamism, opposed to shrinking back.

(c) Heb 11:1–40. Excursus on faith

According to the author, christian existence is dynamic, that is, it is orientated towards the future, the end (cf 3:14; 6:11). The church, God's people (cf 3:9), is on the move, a pilgrim people marching exodus-wise (cf 3:7–4:11) through the desert of this world towards the heavenly Jerusalem (cf 8:1) into which Jesus has already entered as our pioneer or forerunner (cf 2:10; 6:20, 12:2). Hence the primary christian virtues are faithfulness, hope, confidence, endurance, patience and perseverance (cf 3:6, 14; 6:11; 10:23, 36). By these virtues the christian tends towards the future, towards what is not seen or experienced immediately (cf Rom 8:24–25). In 10:38, however, evoking Hab 2:3–4, the author has suggested that christian existence also has a vital, actual and existential character. Totally directed towards the future, it has nevertheless a root in the present. The christian lives by faith (cf 10:38; Rom 1:17; Gal 3:11). He already possesses by faith what he is moving towards by hope. Faith is the actualisation, the rendering present of God's promises. By faith the christian transcends the phenomena of this world and the successive events of history, and already grasps the *eschaton*, the end (1:1).

In 6:12f the author exhorted his readers to imitate the faith of their ancestors, as opposed to the disbelief of the generation of the desert (cf 3:7–4:11). He now takes up and elaborates this point (11:2–40). All the great men of Israel were men of faith (11:2, 39). Just as we, by faith, perceive the invisible God beyond what we see and experience (11:3; cf Rom 1:19–20), so they, by faith, saw beyond the immediate present to a future which God had in store for them. They relied on God's promise of a reward (11:6; cf 10:35) and lived as if it were already realised. The whole of this chapter forms a kind of pendant to 3:7–4:11 in which faith is opposed to disbelief. Faith is presented not as the acceptance of a set of truths but as complete obedience to and absolute dependence

upon God's word, despite apparent contradiction, difficulties, and trials.

(d) Heb 12:1–11. Exhortation to shun sin and to persevere

The most eloquent witness to the need for, and the value
of, faith and perseverance is Jesus himself 'the pioneer
(cf 2:10; 6:20) and perfecter of our faith' (cf 2:17;
3:2–6), since he did not merely look forward to the end,
without actually attaining it, as the old testament heroes.
By his heavenly exaltation he has achieved fulfilment, has
been made perfect (12:1–2; cf 2:10; 5:9). He, therefore,
is the example to be followed in the struggle against sin
(12:3–4; cf 12:1).

In 2:10–18 the author stressed more the ontological
aspect of the christian's divine sonship in the Son. Now he
emphasises its moral aspect. The sufferings of the human
condition, especially the struggle to lead a life of virtue
(12:1, 4), are a form of discipline, a means of education
in true filial piety (cf 5:7). Just as Christ, even though
he was a son (5:8), learned obedience through his sufferings and achieved fulfilment (5:9), so the christian as a
son in the Son must follow the same path to fulfilment.
He must learn to detect the loving, educative hand of
God, his Father, in all the sufferings of his life, and accept
them as Christ did. We must share in Christ's sufferings if
we wish to share in his holiness (12:5–11; 2:11, 14; Rom
8:17).

(e) Heb 12:12–13. Encouragement

Having given the christian interpretation of his readers'
sufferings (cf 12:5–11), the author now encourages them
to take new heart.

(f) Heb 12:14–17. Exhortation to virtue

Positively, the refreshment and renewal of 12:12–13 consist in the pursuit of virtue (12:14–16). While the author allows for the healing of 'drooping hands', 'weak knees' and lameness (12:12–13), he re-affirms that there is no possibility of repentance for the person who has decidedly rejected his inheritance (12:17; cf 1:14; 6:4–8; 10:26–31).

(g) Heb 12:18–24. Sinai and the heavenly Jerusalem

In 8:1–5 the author opposed the heavenly sanctuary and Christ's heavenly liturgy to those of judaism here evoked by the reference to Sinai (12:18–21). Now he stresses that all christians have access to the heavenly city (12:22; cf 11:10, 16) and have thus obtained the fulfilment promised to their ancestors (cf 11:39–40). Christian faith is related not simply to a future reality as was the faith of the old testament. It is access to a present reality, that is, Christ's paschal mystery, although even this has a futuristic aspect, its final manifestation in Christ's second appearance (cf 9:28; 10:38, 25). The christian already enjoys the presence of God in, through and with Christ. The superiority of the christian liturgy over that of the old testament is itself a source of great encouragement.

(h) Heb 12:25–29. Exhortation not to neglect God's word

The excellence of the new covenant (cf 12:24) demands a response more serious than that envisaged in the old testament (12:25; cf 2:1–4), and God's judgement is infinitely more penetrating in the new covenant than in the old (12:29; cf 4:12–13). The present kingdom in which

the christian shares (cf 12:18–24) is God's definitive, un-
shakeable kingdom for which we must be grateful and in
which we can and must offer acceptable worship to God
(12:26–28). The whole aim of christian existence, the
raison d'être of the new testament, the purpose of Christ's
paschal mystery, is the worship of the living God (cf
12:22; 9:14). Christ's priesthood reaches its fulfilment
in the christian's priesthood.

*1. Discuss how Hebrews spiritualises the old testament
liturgical ideas.*

*2. How far does Hebrews reflect historical circum-
stances?*

3. Discuss Hebrews' notion of faith.

*4. In what sense does the resisting of temptation in-
volve a fight?*

*5. How does the author see the relation between the
church and the old testament community?*

6. Discuss the eschatology of Hebrews.

8
Epilogue
Heb 13:1–25

(a) Heb 13:1–19. Exhortations

Having exhorted his readers to offer to God acceptable worship (cf 12:28), the author now proceeds, in a series of practical recommendations, to describe in what precisely this consists (cf 13:15–17): love, hospitality, works of mercy (13:1–3), purity (13:4), detachment from wealth (13:5–6). The leaders of the community merit a double mention (13:7, 17). Those of the past (13:7; cf 2:3) are to be remembered as models of faith (cf 6:12; 11:1–40). But, as in 6:19–20 and 12:2, the readers are reminded that Jesus Christ is the only perfect model of faith (13:8). All the others are dead but he is the same yesterday, that is, during his earthly life (cf 5:7) and at his death and resurrection (cf 9:14), today, that is, exalted at God's right hand (cf 1:3), and forever, that is, eternally making intercession for us (cf 7:25).

Just as Christ's death involved a rupture from the old testament sacrificial system, the abrogation of the Jewish liturgy (cf 9:8), so the christian must be divorced from the peculiarities of judaism, whether these be of alimentary laws (13:9) or temple worship (13:10–13). After Christ's death, there is only one altar, that is, Christ himself (13:10). He has assumed the role formerly played by the temple, sacrifices and priesthood. The fact that Jesus'

47

sacrificial death occurred outside the temple and Jerusalem was itself a sign both that these had lost their profound religious significance and that those who follow
Jesus (cf 2:10) must also leave judaism, the abuse which
necessarily follows being a share in Christ's ignominy
(13:13; cf 12:2). But this exit from judaism is only one
example of the exodus structure of the whole of christian
existence. The christian has no resting place in this world,
no city (13:14; cf 3:7–4:11; 11:10, 16; 12:22). Since
Christ is our altar (13:10) it is through him that we offer
our sacrifice of praise (13:15). With the abrogation of all
animal sacrifices there is now only one sacrifice, that of
praise (cf Ps 50:14, 23), which is the unique, eternal
sacrifice of Christ (cf 7:25), acknowledged by the confession of faith (cf 3:1; 4:14 cf 1 Pet 2:5). Living faith, the
acceptance of the total human situation, in the spirit of
the faithful Christ (cf 2:17; 3:2–6) is the only true christian worship (cf 9:14). This faith, however, must issue as
service of others, just as Christ assumed the total human
situation for all (cf 2:9). The sacrifices pleasing to God
(cf 12:28) are not simply words but also actions: doing
good and sharing one's goods (13:16). The eternity of
Christ's sacrifice (cf 9:14) has as its effect the sacrificial
character of the whole of christian existence (cf 2:11).

The second mention of leaders (13:17; cf 13:7) concerns obedience and is an important reference to the
hierarchical structure of the readers' community (cf
13:24).

As Paul in his letters, the author asks his readers for
their prayers in his regard (13:18–19).

(b) Heb 13:20–21. Blessing

This brief passage resumes the essential message of the

whole work. In 13:15-16 the author has exhorted his readers to offer to God acceptable sacrifices through Jesus Christ. Now he prays that God may effect this in them. The end of christian existence is to give glory to God, by sharing in God's glory (cf 2:10). This has been achieved by God in the paschal mystery of his Son (cf 2:9; 9:14) and it will be realised in us, in so far as the same God unites us to his paschal mystery and makes us share in his priesthood.

(c) Heb 13:22-25. Final exhortation, personal news and blessing

The expression 'word of exhortation' (13:22) gives an important clue to the understanding of the whole work. The reference to Timothy (13:23) has been taken mistakenly as an indication of the pauline origin of the work. The allusion to the 'leaders and all the saints' (13:24) is again a reflection of the hierarchical structure of the community (cf 13:17). The mention of Italy (ibid), tells us nothing definite about the origin or the destination of the work. Finally, the work ends with a typically epistolary blessing, thus giving it at least the appearance of a letter.

1. Show how Hebrews identifies the christian's sacrifice with his life in the world.

2. How does the author's prayer synthesise his work?

3. What does the end of the work tell us about its author and his main aim?

9

General conclusion

As most of the other new testament writings, Hebrews was written for a specific purpose. It is obviously dated by the author's immediate horizon, mentality, culture, mode of argument and the problems he wished to tackle. Nevertheless, this 'word of exhortation' has an abiding message. One might say that never since it was first delivered, nearly two thousand years ago, has it had as much relevance as it has for us today.

Faith, faithfulness, hope and confidence amidst the radical and perplexing changes of an age—this is the essential message of Hebrews. For its original readers this meant a rupture from the familiar and comforting cultic structures of judaism and adherence to the more austere demands of Christ. It meant a decisive leap in the dark, a perpetual wandering around the desert of this world with Christ as the only guide. The christian today also lives in an age of marked transition, even of revolution. No revolution will ever be as shattering as that which shook the world in Christ in the first century of our era. But we are still living within this revolution. For us it is not a question of abandoning the levitical structures of a pre-christian era. It is rather a matter of resisting the perennial temptation to reduce christianity to such structures, or to prop up our lives with anything that is not

Christ. It is far from coincidental that the Jewish cultic apparatus so clearly and resolutely denounced by Hebrews as obsolete and superseded by the unique Christ-event has, for centuries past, influenced the way christians have thought about and described this event. The exodus demanded of the faithful christian today is just as radical as that required of the judaeo-christians of the first century. It is in fact the same exodus.

Whether Hebrews was written before or after the fall of Jerusalem and the destruction of the temple in 70 AD, it must have been a profound source of consolation and encouragement to all those who, in the face of these events, must have thought that the world had come to an end. What this work did for the christians of the Mediterranean of the 70's it can do also for all the christians in the topsy-turvy world of the 1970's.

1. *Outline the main themes of Hebrews, showing their interconnection.*

2. *What is the message of Hebrews to the christian of the twentieth century?*

The pastoral epistles

Jerome Smith

Introduction

The pastoral epistles face us with a difficult conundrum: how on earth did St Paul come to change so his whole mind and personality, as well as his style, by the time he came to write them? Or if someone else wrote them, what on earth was he doing inventing all those personal details about Paul's journeyings, imprisonment, friends, enemies, even his cloak, scrolls and note-books? It may be true of some of the letters that problems of dating and authenticity don't seem important—on any view of those Ephesians constitutes a great theological affirmation. But the pastorals offer us some liturgical fragments, the beginnings—rather pedestrian beginnings—of a church order, and some scrappy sets of personal notes and jottings about people and places we spoke of just now. Even with the authority of Paul's name behind them we shall put them in the margin of his contribution to the new testament; without it, we shall move them firmly to the periphery of new testament statements, leaving the centre to the gospels, the great Paulines, and Hebrews.

But which? This is not the place for yet another rehearsing of the arguments for and against. It is the place for a clear-cut decision, with just a sketch of how it was arrived at. This commentary will stand on a decision that St Paul is not the author of the pastorals and that they were written a generation after his death. My main reason for saying this is that there is a decisive shift in

attitude towards the coming of Christ when we compare
the pastorals with the great Paulines, and it is possible to
put one's finger on a clear contradiction in practical teaching that embodies this basic shift. In 1 Cor 7 St Paul
answers questions put to him on marriage and celibacy.
What he has to say about widows there plainly contradicts
the teaching of the pastorals.

> To the unmarried and the widows I say that it is well
> for them to remain single as I do. But if they cannot
> exercise self-control, they should marry. For it is better
> to marry than to be aflame with passion. 1 Cor 7:8–9.

> Let a widow be enrolled if she is not less than sixty
> years of age, having been the wife of one husband. . . .
> But refuse to enroll younger widows; for when they
> grow wanton against Christ they desire to marry, and
> so they incur condemnation for having violated their
> first pledge. 1 Tim 5:9. 11–12.

In 1 Corinthians St Paul's hope is that everyone should
remain in his or her present state; for the unmarried this
has the special advantage that they can devote themselves
to the Lord undividedly. Celibacy for the Lord's sake is a
personal and individual gift within the community, and
individuals retain their freedom to marry or not to marry
at all times. The situation in the pastorals is quite
different: there is an 'order' of enrolled widows, analogous
in some ways to later religious orders. Widows who have
the necessary entrance qualifications are free to seek
enrolment or not, but once enrolled they may not marry,
on pain of public wantonness and violation of pledge.
This was judged too severe a discipline for young widows
and so they were told to marry and have children, 1 Tim
5:14.

Now there is a clear contradiction there. What is more, the whole motivation and mentality are different. In 1 Corinthians the great point about remaining as you are is that there is not enough time for it to be sensible to do otherwise: 'I think that in view of the impending distress it is well for a person to remain as he is.' 'I mean, brethren, the appointed time has grown very short.' 'For the form of this world is passing away.' 1 Cor 7:26, 29a, 31b. St Paul was clearly wrong about the quantitative shortness of the time left, and it may be that he modified his opinion about that. But in all his genuine writings there is an unmistakable sharp expectancy of Christ's coming that qualifies the whole of his theology and his whole picture of christian living. In the pastorals the sharpness and the urgency have gone, and sensible, practical rules are given about widows without any reference at all to Christ's coming.

That passage on widows is for me a test case for the authorship of the pastorals. And the classic conservative reply to such difficulties does not seem to fit here: that Paul had changed his secretary and left more to his discretion than he had used to. The whole situation is different, the whole mentality different. Any secretary who could do that to St Paul without his knowledge is no longer a mere secretary, but above all he is writing to a new situation that must have taken decades to develop. The sharp expectation of Christ's coming and the meaning of Pauline celibacy cannot have changed so radically in the short space of Paul's last years. The church for which the pastorals were written reckons with its own continuance through an indefinite period of time: as the man Christ Jesus came to ransom mankind at the appointed time, so he will appear again in God's good time, 1 Tim 2:6 and 6:15. New institutions, the priest-bishops and the order of widows, were set up to carry the church through this period of history.

This solution has to stand up to the question raised by the biographical notes and personal jottings attributed to St Paul in 2 Timothy and Titus. Would a student of St Paul writing in a Pauline church invent the details found in 2 Tim 4:9–21? I think the probabilities are against it, and that it is a genuine fragment from St Paul. If that is so, then it would have been added out of piety, not cleverness: if unknown it could authenticate nothing; if known, then it was known not to belong to 2 Timothy.

Book list

1. *A commentary on the Pastoral Epistles* (in Black's *New Testament Commentaries*), J. N. D. Kelly. Dr Kelly believes that St Paul wrote the pastorals, and gives a lucid and careful exposition from that stand-point.

2. *The Pastoral letters* (in *The Cambridge Bible Commentary*), A. T. Hanson. Dr Hanson takes the more usual view that the pastorals were written after St Paul's death, in the first years of the second century, in fact. This series uses the NEB for the English text.

1

Timothy's task
1 Tim 1:1–20

1 Tim 1:1–2. The address

The standard first century form of address at the head of
a letter was: N to N, greeting. This formula was often
slightly expanded, perhaps to define the relationship between the one addressed and the writer, perhaps to offer
a prayer on their behalf. In the new testament letters,
with the exception of James, 'greeting' becomes 'grace',
'grace and peace' and variations upon these. In the great
Paulines, and more especially in Galatians and Romans,
the address becomes quite elaborate and Paul's claim to
apostolic authority is emphasised. There is an echo of that
claim here, 'an apostle by command of God', where Paul's
word is normally 'an apostle by the *will* of God', eg 2 Cor
1:1.

More significantly, God is here called 'God our saviour'.
This is, of course, part of the old testament concept of
God: 'God of Israel, the saviour', Is 45:15. But 'saviour'
is never used of God in the certain Paulines, and its
occurrence here reflects not so much the old testament
concept as the contemporary Greek religious language,
and in particular the use of 'saviour' in the developing
cult of the Roman emperors. Christianity stands con-
sciously over against emperor worship, though care is

taken over the duty of prayer for kings and Caesars, 1 Tim
2 : 1–3. God is called 'saviour' six times in the pastorals.

The letter is addressed to 'Timothy, my true child in
the faith'. We know quite a lot about Timothy, one of
St Paul's closest and most trusted fellow workers. His
grandmother's name was Lois, his mother's Eunice; she
was a Jewess, in spite of her Greek name, but no fanatic,
since she married a pagan Greek and had not bothered
to have her son circumcised. (2 Tim 1 : 5; Ac 16 : 1–3.)
His home was at Lystra in Lycaonia (south central
Turkey) and it was there that St Paul recruited him as a
missionary, being careful to have him circumcised, as
the law commanded for the son of a Jewish mother. Paul
kept him with him on his missionary journeyings, associated him with himself in the address of several of the
letters (1 and 2 Thess, 2 Cor, Phil, Col and Phm), and
sent him on a number of important missions. It is in connection with plans for one of those that we have St Paul's
fullest account of what Timothy meant to him:

I hope in the Lord Jesus to send Timothy to you soon,
so that I may be cheered by news of you. I have no one
like him, who will be genuinely anxious for your welfare. They all look after their own interests, not those
of Jesus Christ. But Timothy's worth you know, how
as a son with a father he has served with me in the
gospel. (Phil 2 : 19–22)

Timothy was with Paul in Rome(?) during his imprisonment there, Phm 1 : 1; his memory was clearly treasured
in the churches of the east where he had worked with
St Paul and perhaps also after his death. The picture of
Timothy as delegate and successor, at least in part, of the
apostle at Ephesus, with a special authority over the whole
church there, ordainer and judge of the local presbyters,

1 Tim 5:19, 22; 2 Tim 2:2, may well reflect a genuine local tradition and provide us with a momentary glimpse of an important stage in the development of the ordained regular ministry.

1. Do you believe that St Paul wrote 1 Timothy? What difference does it make if he didn't? What kind of authority would a non-genuine 1 Timothy have?

2. What kind of claim do bishops have to be successors of people like Timothy, and through him of the apostles themselves? How far is the church today bound to the pattern of bishops, priests and deacons that emerged only after the time of the pastorals? How far is the church free to go back to ordaining local family men for the ministry?

3. Would you agree that some clericalist conservatives and some successful revolutionaries take a quasi-sacral view of state authority? Do you think that the statement of 1 Timothy that God, not Caesar, is saviour has any relevance here?

1 Tim 1:3–7. Myths and genealogies

Timothy is presented to us as Paul's delegate, left at Ephesus to guard against the introduction of strange teachings that are no part of the gospel nor of the traditional teaching of the church: gospel and tradition are one for the writer of the pastorals. The church at Ephesus was founded by St Paul; it was from there that he wrote 1 Corinthians (see 16:8). We are told in Ac 19:8–10 that St Paul spent more than two years there; and apparently Timothy was with him during that time, Ac 19:22, and was sent on ahead of Paul into Macedonia. 1 Timothy does not fit into the situation described in Ac 19, but it does draw upon the known connection between Paul, Timothy and Ephesus.

The strange teachings that Timothy has to deal with consist of myths and endless genealogies. It has often been supposed that this is directed against gnostic systems of the kind attacked by Irenaeus and other fathers of the church from the second century onwards. Gnosticism taught a secret doctrine of emanations from the one divine source, with a fall into material, evil being somewhere along the line, and the despatch of a divine saviour to rescue the souls imprisoned in matter. In christian gnosticism Christ was identified with the divine saviour. Full-blown gnosticism of that kind does not seem to be the problem in the pastorals. In 1:7 here these mythologists are said to want to be teachers of the law, and clearly the OT law is meant. In Tit 1:10, 14, false teachers are again sharply rebuked, and there they are said to belong especially to the circumcision party and to be concerned with Jewish myths. The genealogies here are not emanations in Greek philosophical style but OT genealogies worked up into Jewish myths. The book of Jubilees, originally written in Hebrew in the second century BC, retells the story of Genesis and the first part of Exodus with an admixture of fictitious genealogies and legendary materials. It is probably that kind of 'speculations' that the pastorals take exception to.

These speculations are contrasted with divine training or, reading another word in the Greek manuscripts, stewardship or order. The writer may be contrasting mere fables and legends with God's ordering of human affairs, the true, biblical history of salvation. More likely he opposes them to stewardship exercised under God and for God in the community, which comes to much the same thing as divine training. Paul is more often than not in the thick of an argument, and some of his finest pieces of rhetoric and sheer hard thinking spring out of controversy, for example his theology of law and grace, faith and works, created in response to the challenge of the judaisers. There is little of that in the pastorals: 'disputes about words' (1 Tim 6:4) are countered by an appeal to discipline, good order and tradition.

The great point and aim of christian instruction is simply love. Here Paul's great praise of love in 1 Cor 13 comes at once to mind. For Paul faith and love are two necessary ways of looking at the one basic gift of God: faith denotes especially the beginning of the process, man's sheer openness to God which is itself God's gift, and therefore it is faith that works through love (Gal 5:6). Here in 1 Tim there is a shift in thought as in language: sincere faith is listed in the last place along with pure heart and good conscience, and the three together point to a well-ordered christian life. Something of the glory and the drama of Paul's thinking has been lost: he constantly praised the greatness of God's gift, 'you were washed, you were sanctified, you were justified', 1 Cor 6:11, and then goes on to coax and cajole his converts to struggle after goodness: 'Shall I therefore take the members of Christ and make them members of a prostitute?' 1 Cor 6:15.

At 1:7 we are told that the false teachers want to be teachers of the law. We have seen that the Jewish law is meant; but does this mean that these christian people wanted to be recognised as official Jewish scribes? That would have been unlikely enough even in Paul's later years, in towns where there were Pauline churches and Jewish communities; after the shock of the fall of Jerusalem and formal excommunication of christians from the synagogue it would have been quite impossible. It would appear that the word is used ironically here, to refer to those who set themselves up as 'rabbis' within christian communities.

1. How do you think we ought to react to 'false teaching' today? Is an appeal to authority and tradition enough?

2. What do you think our attitude should be towards 'Jesus freaks', pentecostalists, followers of Zen and so on?

3. Some, at least, of these Jewish christian teachers would have regarded themselves as the true guardians of tradition. How should we treat our own super-traditionalists?

1 Tim 1:8–11. The use of the law

The ironical reference to teachers of the law might suggest a negative attitude to the law itself; the writer is quick to put in a short digression on the proper use of the law to make sure that we do not misunderstand him. Paul himself stated that 'the law is holy, and the commandment is holy and just and good', Rom 7:12, but that was because Paul had just said that sin makes use of the law in order to stimulate our evil desires. Paul could hardly have talked about using the law lawfully, that is, using it to guide our obedience. For him the usefulness of the law is that it convicts us of sin and shows us our need of God's grace. Grace sets us free from the law though, looking at it from another way, love is the fulfilment of the law (Rom 13:10). Paul's dialectic of sin, law and grace is fairly complicated, and it is no wonder that 1 Tim takes a different view. It is important to see just how different it is: for Paul the law is laid down for all, Rom 2:12–14, because no-one is just till God has justified him, Rom 3:20, all are lawless and disobedient, ungodly and sinners; for 1 Tim it is not laid down for the just.

The highly coloured list of sins (more precisely, of sinners) which follows is reminiscent of the one in 1 Cor 6:9–10. There Paul emphasised that some of the Corinthian congregation had really been like that; 1 Tim seems to be addressed to an altogether more 'respectable' audience. The list seems to follow the order of the ten commandments: sodomy was considered to fall under the prohibition of adultery. 'Thou shalt not steal' very likely did refer originally to stealing men into slavery. These sins are contrary to sound doctrine, as are all the others. Sound doctrine is a favourite phrase in the pastorals; it fits in very well with the other indications of a respectable class of people bound firmly together under the tradition and discipline of the church.

This statement about the use of the law is now said to be in accordance with the glorious gospel that has been entrusted to 'Paul'. In 2 Cor 4:4 the 'gospel of glory' is the gospel of the glory of Christ; here the 'gospel of glory' is said to be the glorious gospel of God, but somehow the 'good news' has come to be understood as sound doctrine and the glory has been dimmed. This is not so much any fault in the author as simply the attrition of time; the moral is that if we wish to recapture the freshness of the gospel we should go back to the letters of St Paul.

1. Paul, Matthew and the writer of the pastorals seem to have quite different ways of reading the OT law; do you think we can learn something from these different approaches?

2. How important is sound moral doctrine in christian education?

1 Tim 1:12-17. God's grace towards Paul

Mention of the fact that Paul has been entrusted with the gospel introduces very naturally a fuller account of his conversion and a theological reflection upon its meaning. This account is modelled upon those to be found in Gal 1 and in 1 Cor 15:8-10. For St Paul his vocation as a christian and his vocation as an apostle coincided: God revealed his Son to Paul in order that he might preach him among the gentiles, Gal 1:16. Paul always had a very vivid sense of the greatness of the gift and how little he had deserved it: 'Last of all, as to one untimely born, he appeared also to me. For I am the least of the apostles, unfit to be called an apostle, because I persecuted the church of God.' 1 Cor 15:8-9.

There is a natural and well-known tendency, reported from revivalist meetings, group therapy sessions and so on, for people to give highly-coloured accounts of their own wickednesses: if we cannot excel as saints at least we can do better as sinners than others! In 1 Corinthians St Paul seems to have this temptation under control, here in 1 Timothy he would seem to have let it run away with him, if he had written it himself: 'I am the foremost of sinners'. But if 1 Timothy is written by one of Paul's disciples, or by a disciple of a disciple, then this exaggeration is quite understandable. So too is the excuse: Paul had not tried to excuse himself by saying that he had acted out of ignorance, though that was, of course, perfectly true; it is entirely proper for a disciple to do so. This theological interpretation is a splendid reflection of Paul's own teaching on sin and grace: 'where sin increased, grace abounded all the more', Rom 5:20. As Paul was the greatest of sinners, so too he is the greatest exemplar of the perfect patience of Christ towards sinners. (It would be more in St Paul's style to speak of *God*'s patience with sinners, Rom 2:4; 9:22.) Where Paul's sin of persecution had increased, the grace of Christ had abounded all the more, overflowing with faith and love.

1:15 contains a phrase: 'The saying is sure' that occurs four more times in the pastorals, 1 Tim 3:1; 4:9; 2 Tim 2:11; Tit 3:8. 1 Tim 3:1 is a puzzle that we can leave till we get there; the others seem to be short, or fairly short, sayings about the relationship between present christian existence and the life in Christ to come or, as here, about the purpose of the incarnation. It is very likely that they belong to a collection of christian maxims or proverbs that sum up, from a particular angle, the essence of christian faith.

The paragraph ends with a doxology, a prayer of praise modelled upon those that punctuate Paul's own letters, eg Rom 1:25; Phil 4:20. They are a characteristic of rabbinical style; at any mention of God the phrase 'Blessed be he!' is likely to bubble up spontaneously. There are two points about this doxology. It is a mixture of Jewish and Greek styles: God is the 'king of ages' as in Tobit 13:6: 'Praise the Lord of righteousness, and exalt the King of ages'; he is also the incorruptible and invisible one, as in Greek religious language. St Paul mixes his styles in just this way, eg in his quotation from Ps 106 in Rom 1:23, they 'changed the glory of the incorruptible God (where Paul has added "incorruptible God") for images resembling mortal man or birds or animals or reptiles.' More importantly, the starting point for the doxology is the mention of Jesus Christ, but since his patience with sinners is ultimately his Father's patience, there follows immediately the doxology addressed to the invisible Father. There is a mention of Christ followed by a doxology at Rom 9:5, and there is an argument as to whether Christ or the Father is there addressed as God. There is no doubt that the Father is meant here.

    1. How useful do you think is the advice always to think of yourself as least worthy of God's love?

    2. How far should our liturgical prayers express our personal feelings of guilt?

1 Tim 1:18–20. Timothy's commission

The charge or instructions given to Timothy imply a commission with which he is entrusted: it will involve him in directing all teaching in the community and in giving instructions (charges: the verb in 1 : 3 and the noun here in 1 : 18 are different forms of the same word in Greek) to the teachers of strange doctrines to stop that and return to the teaching of sound doctrine (1 : 10). This commission, which Paul is said to be renewing through this letter, was given to Timothy on an earlier occasion when christian prophets pointed to him as the man for the job. Christian prophecy is mentioned again in connection with Timothy and his work at 4 : 14, where it goes with a laying on of hands in a commissioning ceremony. The church for which 1 Timothy was written was clearly one in which christian prophecy still played a functional role: even the choice of church officials depended upon the working of the gifts of the Spirit. Though the church revealed in the pastorals is much more institutionalised than the church of 1 and 2 Corinthians, it remains still at essential points a charismatic community.

    One of St Paul's favourite images for missionary work is soldiering, and he was even willing, on occasion, to use it in the context of struggle within the christian community:

Though we live in the world we are not carrying on a worldly war, for the weapons of our warfare are not worldly but have divine power to destroy strongholds. We destroy arguments and every proud obstacle to the knowledge of God, and take every thought captive to obey Christ, being ready to punish every disobedience, when your obedience is complete. 2 Cor 10:3–6.

But Paul produced that statement in answer to the accusation that he was bold and courageous in his letters, while humble and gentle face to face; there wasn't much of the ruthless Roman military mind about him. The echo of 2 Corinthians comes in aptly here, for Timothy too is faced with disobedience in the community. Some people thought he was too young for the job, 1 Tim 4:12.

Timothy is told to hold on to faith and good conscience, in contrast to those who have rejected conscience and so wrecked their faith. Here again, as in 1:5, we meet with that near identification of faith with a good life. Faith is a matter of sound doctrine directly tied to a sound moral way of life; to turn away from the community discipline of ethical practice involves destruction of the pattern of moral values inherent in christian teaching.

Two of the false teachers are named. Hymenaeus is presumably the same man mentioned in 2 Timothy along with Philetus for giving out false doctrine about the resurrection, 2:17. Alexander was a common name, and this one has no obvious connection with Alexander the Jewish spokesman of Ac 19:33; perhaps Alexander the coppersmith and great opponent of Paul's teaching, 2 Tim 4:14–15, would fit the bill. If these two names of excommunicates come down from Paul's time, then it is likely that their disciples are still active; but perhaps these excommunicates belong to the same generation as the

writer of the pastorals. Paul had trouble over incest at
Corinth, and gave instructions for the excommunication
of the guilty one, whom, quite typically, he did not name:

> Though absent in body I am present in spirit, and as if
> present, I have already pronounced judgment in the
> name of the Lord Jesus on the man who has done such a
> thing. When you are assembled, and my spirit is
> present, with the power of our Lord Jesus, you are to
> deliver this man to Satan for the destruction of the
> flesh, that his spirit may be saved in the day of the Lord
> Jesus. 1 Cor 5 : 3–5.

The meaning of the excommunication here is much the
same, for the word 'learn', literally 'to treat like a child',
is a grim one, used to refer to our Lord's scourging in
Luke's passion story (23 : 16, 22), and for beating to death
in Paul's list of paradoxes in 2 Cor 6 : 8b–10, 'punished,
and yet not killed'. And affliction by God, some deadly
sickness, is what is meant here, for false teaching is blas-
phemy against God. This kind of attitude to heresy and
heretics was to have all too successful a run in the church,
and where God's afflictions were lacking men's were not:
this is the starting-point of the mediaeval inquisition.

*1. Do you think we ought to give greater scope in the
church to prophecy and the gifts of the Spirit? What forms
could this take?*

*2. How should the church respond nowadays to false
teaching and attempts to justify immoral practice? Who
is going to decide which is which, and how?*

2

Order in the church
1 Tim 2:1–3:13

1 Tim 2:1–7. Prayer to be made for all men

Timothy's commission was particularly concerned with teaching in the community, for it was essentially a believing community founded upon a definite structure of belief concerning God's action in Christ; and, as we shall see, teaching is the primary concern of the community officials. But faith issues in confession and prayer, as also in action; the teachers of faith are therefore leaders in prayer, and the writer lays down some general rules for this.

The church of the pastorals is the house of God, the pillar and bulwark of the truth established by God in this world, 1 Tim 3:15, and has therefore a universal scope. But the impression we get of the actual circumstances and living conditions of the community is quite modest and domestic. The community depends in an essential way upon the personal virtues of its officers in their own households as in the church at large; there is a special emphasis upon the duty of hospitality for them as also among candidates for the order of widows (1 Tim 3:2; Tit 1:8; 1 Tim 5:10). The general impression is one of small face-to-face groups scattered among the non-christian population in the towns. They were not exempt from the temptation typical of small groups and sects, that of retreating within the walls of their own ghettos in exclusion of and even enmity towards those outside. These tendencies were strengthened and exaggerated by the false teachers with their interest in strange and secret Jewish myths.

Against this kind of sectarian temptation 1 Timothy gives a firm reminder of the fundamental christian duty of prayer for all men universally, which is founded upon the unity and universality of God, and upon his work for the salvation of all mankind through Christ Jesus. Christians are to give thanks to God on behalf of all men (above all, surely, at the eucharist itself), and intercession is to be made for all, and especially for rulers. The 'kings' mentioned here are probably, in the first place, the Roman emperor and those associated with him: co-regent, if any, designated successor and the principal imperial officials. Nothing in the pastorals suggests that they were written in a time of sharp persecution, but Jesus' own death 'under Pontius Pilate', sporadic persecutions from the time of Nero onwards, the great Jewish war of 66–70 and its aftermath provided constant occasion for anti-imperial bitterness and hatred. 1 Timothy follows faithfully Paul's teaching in Rom 13: the authority of the state is instituted by God and must be accepted and the holders prayed for. Obedience and prayer make for a quiet life, and a quiet life makes room for religion and decency. This is a rather unheroic ideal of christian life, but it goes with a firm grasp of the universal meaning of the gospel.

It is right to pray for all men and be at peace with all because that is in keeping with the will of God, who is the saviour of all christians and wills to be saviour of all men without exception. All should come to acknowledge the truth of the gospel and become members of the church, instructed in her basic catechism, 'the knowledge of the truth' spoken of also in Heb 10:26. Salvation outside the visible institution of the church is not yet conceived of, but the gospel centres upon the unity of God and the totality of the redemption in and through Christ. 'There is one God, and there is one mediator between God and men, the man Christ Jesus, who gave himself as a ransom for all' is a two-clause creed of a similar pattern to the one in 1 Cor 8:6. It is very natural that 1 Timothy should quote a traditional prayer in the context of giving instructions about prayer. There are many passages in the pastorals with a liturgical ring about them, and they contain the deepest theological statements to be found in these letters.

The central word that defines Christ's position and work here, 'mediator', is a rich and weighty one that has an essential place in the development of the church's doctrine. It is found three times over in Hebrews, where Jesus is the mediator of the new and greater covenant (Heb 8:6; 9:15; 12:24). Connected as it is with the great NT theme of the covenant between God and men in Christ, it expresses a way of looking at Christ's work very like Paul's own. By a quirk of vocabulary and his inherited rabbinical logic Paul uses the word only in a contorted argument in Galatians to show that the law, which was given through a mediator (Moses?), is inferior to the promise, which was given directly (Gal 3:19–20). Christ is mediator in and through his death, the covenant sacrifice, and this, in turn, evokes the theme of Christ's blood the price of redemption, 'who gave himself as a ransom for all' (cf 1 Cor 6:20; Rom 3:24; Mk 10:15).

The phrase about the 'testimony' is tacked on to the confessional statement in a rather puzzling way. The RSV 'the testimony to which' seems to presuppose that someone else has testified to the redemptive death of Christ, perhaps Paul by his preaching. But if the word 'to' is omitted, and it is not in the Greek, then the phrase would run 'the testimony which was borne at the proper time' and would refer to Christ's death in testimony to God's intention to redeem and to save. 1 Tim 6:13 speaks of Christ Jesus giving testimony before Pontius Pilate, which may well refer to the death on the cross as well as to the trial scene. Christ's witness to God on the cross is the necessary foundation for apostolic witness and preaching; and Paul's office as teacher of the gentiles (cf Gal 2:7–9) reflected the universality of the redemption.

1. What should our attitude be towards the state and those in any kind of authority over us?

2. What do you think of the ideal of a peaceful and religious life sketched here?

3. Since God desires all men to be saved, how does this work out in terms of 'knowledge of the truth'?

1 Tim 2:8–15. Women in the church

The writer now moves on from the question 'For whom should we pray?' to 'How should we pray?', to behaviour in the church assembly. The men do not seem to have been a particular problem for him, and so the paragraph is mainly about women in church. It is sufficient, then, to remind the men that prayer is a universal duty that cannot be carried out in a spirit of hatred or anger; we will remember Jesus' instruction in the gospel about breaking off the ceremony even at the point of the offering of sacrifice in order to go first and secure reconciliation, Mt 5:23–4. In ancient times pagans, Jews and christians adopted the same physical stance for prayer: standing up with hands stretched out and open.

Women are clearly something of a problem in this church. They will dress up and distract the men with sexual thoughts; worse still, they refuse to keep silent and set themselves up as teachers and rulers over the men. There is no suggestion that they have been appointed as church officers through an official appointment with laying on of hands; clearly something more spontaneous and charismatic is meant. The women no doubt claimed to be gifted and driven on by the Spirit, and claimed the right to prophesy and teach under his influence. Part of the background to this is a clash of cultures; women had to keep silent in the Jewish synagogues, while prophetesses and priestesses flourished in the hellenistic world. The writer of 1 Timothy takes a Jewish and male view of the question, and appeals to the story of Adam and Eve in Genesis to bear him out. Paul had been faced with a similar problem at Corinth, and had also appealed to the story of Adam and Eve, but the conclusion he drew from it was milder: women must have their heads veiled in the church assembly, even when they pray or prophesy, 1 Cor 11:2–16. It is possible that Paul found the argument from Genesis something less than convincing; certainly his clinching argument is a simple appeal to church tradition. (There is a ruling against women speaking in the church at 1 Cor 14:34–35, but those verses are very likely an addition to the original text; they are put after verse 40 in some manuscripts, they interrupt the sequence of the argument, and they contradict what Paul said in 1 Cor 11.) Paul appeals to Genesis only to establish a relationship of order: as woman was created from man's body, so woman was created for man and is his glory, as he is God's. 1 Timothy brings in the story of the fall as well: Adam was not deceived but the woman was. Now there is a passage in Rom 7 which speaks of commandment, sin, deception and death, where the passage is told in the first person but where Paul seems to be identifying himself with Adam. There it is clearly stated that Adam–Paul was deceived: 'For sin, finding opportunity in the commandment, deceived me and by it killed me.' (7:11.)

Eve seems, in fact, to be altogether a more sinister character here in 1 Timothy as compared with 1 Corinthians. She is a mixture of Eve and Delilah, more highly sexed than man, and likely at any time to lead him into transgression by her sexual wiles. The only hope is for the men to keep her firmly in her place, and for her to accept the destiny laid down for her in Gen 3:16: salvation through child-bearing and chaste obedience. But Eve has, of course, become a christian, so these must spring from christian virtue: faith, love and holiness.

1. What part should lay people play in public prayer? Would it be a good thing for them to lead prayers sometimes? Should prayers always be composed beforehand?

2. Is women's liberation acceptable from a christian point of view? Are there any theological limits to it?

3. Is there any theological reason why women should not be priests and bishops? What about social and cultural reasons?

1 Tim 3:1–13. Bishops and deacons

'The saying is sure' in the opening words of ch 3, but which saying is it? Some commentators, despairing of the bishop, have turned back to woman at the end of ch 2, and tried to find a christian maxim or proverb there. But the other maxims, as we have seen, are concerned with the

relationship between present christian existence and the
life in Christ to come: that is very much latent, if not
buried, in the saying about women. It is simpler to take
the phrase as referring to the bishop after all. It would of
course be even more difficult to find a reference to life
now and life to come in Christ in the statement that anyone wanting to be a bishop is wishing for a good job. But
probably this is not a pre-existent maxim at all; the
pastorals are naturally much concerned with church
officers, and the writer is putting forward a new proverb
of his own to emphasise just how necessary and important
they are.

There is a puzzle about the bishop in the pastorals: he
occurs only in the singular and his relationship to the
elders is never precisely defined. Strictly, the word in 3:1
here is 'episcopacy', but in 3:2 and in Tit 1:7 'bishop'.
These are the only occurrences in the pastorals. 'Elder'
is used three times of church officers, 1 Tim 5:17, 19,
Tit 1:5, and 'presbytery', the office of elder or the body
of elders, once: 1 Tim 4:14. Elders, or some of them,
have the same job as the bishop: ruling, preaching and
teaching. The passage in Tit 1 moves on from speaking
of elders to speak of the bishop as if talking about the
same office. In Ac 20 elders, 20:17, and bishops (RSV
'guardians'), 20:28, are the same people, and that is true
generally of early christian writings in the first and well
into the second century, with the notable exception of the
letters of Ignatius of Antioch from the beginning of the
second century, in which the single ('monarchical') bishop
has emphatically arrived. It has been suggested that the
pastorals have been carefully phrased so as to cover both
the many bishops and the single bishop situations. It is
simpler to suppose that the monarchical bishop has not
yet performed his takeover bid; Timothy and Titus do in

some ways anticipate him, but they may well be figures of past history, and direct and irreplaceable delegates of the apostle Paul. Elders and bishops are probably the same people in the pastorals.

What sort of person, then, should be chosen as bishop-elder, and what kind of functions should he perform? Greek moralists were fond of drawing up lists of virtuous qualities desirable in public functionaries, rulers, generals, doctors, and indeed for virtuous and therefore public men quite generally; A. T. Hanson remarks that the list here is very like one given by Onosander for a general! It is claimed by some contemporary moral philosophers and theologians that christianity offers no special and unique moral teaching, though arguably gives greater depth and perspective to general moral teaching; certainly NT writers were ready to draw upon the commonplaces of hellenistic moral reflection.

Though the qualities listed are commonplace, some of them have a particular relevance. 'Husband of one wife' is totally in keeping with hellenistic theory; the sexual instinct is notoriously difficult to control, while its use is clearly part of family and community, for that matter human, duty. But to involve oneself in this sub-public and sub-philosophical round once death or divorce had set one free was not regarded as a mark of the virtuous man. It was hardly necessary to ask what women thought of the arrangement, even where they had won the right to divorce. In marriage as in everything else, women were expected to accept without question the theories and practices of a world dominated by men. 1 Timothy's arrangements have this much of equality about them: a like condition was exacted of candidates for the enrolled widowhood, 5:9. Women's liberation lay far in the future, and there is no sign that christian women thought of being bishop-elders.

'Hospitable' is a quality worth noting among the (necessary) ethical conditions for church office. J.-P. Audet has shown how essential this was to the growth of the church in the pre-Constantinian centuries. The church was essentially a missionary but domestic, 'religious' yet, by the standards of the age, lay movement. The role of the men and women who kept open house for the meetings of the local christian communities was absolutely crucial, and there are a number of references to them in the epistles: Rom 16:5; Rom 16:23; 1 Cor 16:19; Col 4:15; Philemon 2. They are often found among the first converts in any particular town, and the male heads of such households would regularly have been bishop-elders; Stephanas, for example, mentioned in 1 Cor 16:15–18. Careful scholars have warned us against too romantic a picture of the 'church of the catacombs', quite rightly. Normal church meetings would have taken place in the house-churches, in spite of all the dangers involved for the bishop-elders and hosts. In such circumstances, as throughout times of persecution for the church, hospitality became a qualification for martyrdom. Christians were detested for a sect of atheists, without god or shrine, temple or altar, priesthood or sacrifice; their leaders and linchpins were these 'lay' (I put in the inverted commas to acknowledge the different standards of that time and the development of ritual language in christian tradition) bishop-elders and hosts. Given the domestic character of the local congregations, it is natural that stress should be laid upon family virtues: 'He must manage his own household well, keeping his children submissive and respectful in every way; for if a man does not know how to manage his own household, how can he care for God's church?' The references to drunkenness and love of money have a relevance here too: they were the keepers of the community purse and it was part of their duty to keep a stock of wine for community suppers and eucharists.

The caution against appointing recent converts is a mark of the loss of the first fresh enthusiasm and the bold risk-taking that went with it (just think of the situation at Corinth reflected in 1 Corinthians: everything from incest to drunken eucharists); the church is settling down to the dullness of good administration necessary to the survival of any institution.

Since the church is a community of faith a primary duty of the leaders is serving faith: the bishop-elder must be 'an apt teacher'. This duty runs right through the pastorals, and it is through teaching, above all, that Timothy and Titus function as delegates and colleagues of Paul the 'preacher and apostle and teacher', 2 Tim 1:11. Whether you agree with the theory that Paul is not the author or no, it is clear that the pastorals lay claim to an apostolic succession in teaching (and ruling goes with teaching, 1 Tim 5:17) for the bishop-elders. It has just been suggested that they would have been, very often, hosts to the churches meeting in their houses and concerned with the provision of bread and wine for the eucharist (in Paul's time, apparently, people brought their own and wrongly refused to put it in the common kitty, 1 Cor 11:21); what would have been more natural than for them to preside at the eucharist and, as part of their teaching office, to offer the great prayer of thanksgiving in the name of all. The absence of any clear and precise reference to the eucharist in the pastorals is puzzling; there is perhaps an indirect reference latent here. Teaching certainly meant a retelling of the gospel, a rehearsing of the wonderful works of God in and through Jesus Christ (1 Tim 3:16; 2 Tim 1:8–14; Tit 2:11–15); in OT language this is to bless, to give thanks, to recount, to remember. In the days of extempore eucharistic prayer, when the celebrant gave thanks to the utmost of his ability (Justin Martyr), giving thanks at the eucharist was an essential part of the ministry of the word, entrusted especially to those who stood in the apostolic succession of teaching.

The Greek words from which our 'deacon' and 'diaconate' come are general words for servant and service, as for example in serving at table, and they are applied to Jesus and to his apostles as well as to church servants like Timothy (1 Tim 4:6; 2 Tim 4:5). Here it refers to a special office of assistant to the bishop-elder, in the duties of hospitality (and perhaps therefore at the eucharist) and of care of the common purse, if that is not to read too much into 'not addicted to much wine, not greedy for gain'. There is no mention of a share in teaching; 'they must hold the mystery of the faith with a clear conscience' is something that could be stated of any christian. 'Faith' points to the content of faith, the plan of God formerly hidden in his providence and now revealed and realised in Christ. From the indicative statement of what God has done there follows immediately the imperative command of christian living, hence the phrase 'clear conscience'.

Who are the women mentioned in the middle of this paragraph on deacons? If they are simply deacons' wives, as many think, why is it only after they have been mentioned that the writer goes on to stipulate that the deacons must be 'the husband of one wife'? And the qualities demanded of these women look very much like qualifications for some kind of office. All in all, they are probably deaconesses, probably entrusted with a ministry towards the women of the congregation, in view of the prohibition on women having authority over the men, 2:12. A woman called Phoebe is called deaconess of the church at Cenchreae in Rom 16:1; there is an argument over whether that is a reference to a definite office. Service ('diaconate') is distinguished in Rom 12:6–7 from prophecy and teaching; it may well have been a fairly definite function on its way to becoming an office.

The 'great confidence in the faith' promised to good deacons is a basic christian quality of courage and freedom in speech and action spoken of in both Acts and the Paulines. Here it is not a grace of office; rather, faithful office-holders are promised their share of a necessary and fundamental christian gift.

1. What do you think of the idea of married priests? bishops?

2. Now that we have got back to the idea and reality of permanent deacons, do you think there is a place for deaconesses?

3. What do you think of the unclerical picture of church ministers given here? Do you think the clergy should be men 'set apart' as they are at present? What kind of priests would you like to see?

1 Tim 3:14–16. The church and Christ

After the lists of qualities necessary in bishop-elders and deacons, and before taking up the theme of the false teaching once again in 4:1–10, 'Paul' reminds his readers of what it is all about: the church and Christ. The passage about the bishop-elders and deacons had established an analogy between household and church, 3:5, 12; now the household of God is identified with the church of God.

Both words have OT origins: Moses was entrusted with all
God's house, Num 12:7 quoted at Heb 3:2, 5, the house
that is the people; and the people assembled at Sinai is
called simply *the* assembly, the church, Deut 9:10. Does
this passage in 1 Timothy speak of the local congregation
or of the world-wide church? The echo of the household
and church of 3:5 would suggest that the local church
is meant; the hymn that follows in 3:16, with its reference
to the preaching of the mystery of Christ among the
nations, points rather to the world-wide church. The
church is the pillar and bulwark of the truth over against
the false teachers, who provide a shaky support for un-
stable doctrines; the church as house naturally rests upon
the foundation of Christ, not the other way round.

The fragment of the hymn which follows must originally
have referred back to an explicit mention of Christ; now
he is introduced in a prose phrase as the great mystery of
religion. Religion, piety, is a favourite idea in the
pastorals: christianity is the true religion. The mystery of
God's plan for the world, first hidden in God, then revealed
in word and reality, is an idea inherited in the NT from
OT apocalyptic, eg Dan 2:18, 19. In Col 1:25–27 St Paul
had defined his apostolic role as the preaching of the
mystery of Christ: 'The divine office which was given to
me for you, to make the word of God fully known, the
mystery hidden for ages and generations but now made
manifest to his saints. To them God chose to make known
how great among the Gentiles are the riches of the glory
of this mystery, which is Christ in you.'

The hymn consists of six short phrases, arranged in
pairs containing an inner contrast: flesh-Spirit, angels-
nations, and world-glory. Since angels belong to the divine
world, there is one basic contrast between human and
divine running right through: flesh, nations, world—

Spirit, angels, glory. New testament christological statements all use the contrast. They may be divided into
naive and primitive ones in which the human is assumed
into the divine: 'God has made him both Lord and
Christ, this Jesus whom you crucified', Ac 2:36, and later
and more developed ones in which a pre-existent divine
being submits to a sequence of humiliation and exaltation, as in the great hymn of Phil 2:5b–11, or in Rom
1:3–4: 'his Son, who was descended from David according to the flesh and designated Son of God in power
according to the Spirit of holiness'. That credal passage
from Romans may well have been changed by Paul from
a simple flesh-Spirit contrast to the more elaborate Son-
flesh-spirit sequence. The language of our hymn is
reminiscent of that credal passage and may have undergone a like elaboration from simple flesh-Spirit to mystery-
flesh-Spirit. '[Jesus] who was manifested in the flesh'
would have referred quite simply to the man Jesus living
his human life; now, the mystery who undergoes an
epiphany in the flesh is a divine being who assumes
humanity. The Greek word behind 'manifested' is from
the same verbal root as 'epiphany', and the same idea of
incarnation as epiphany is found at 2 Tim 1:9–10: 'in
virtue of his own purpose and the grace which he gave
us in Christ Jesus ages ago, and now has manifested
through the epiphany of our Saviour Christ Jesus'. God
vindicated his martyr (witness) Jesus in his resurrection-
exaltation; but does 'Spirit' refer to the divine Spirit
which Jesus ultimately is (cf 1 Cor 15:45: 'the last Adam
became a life-giving spirit') or to the Holy Spirit through
whom and into whom Jesus was raised up (cf 'if the Spirit
of him who raised Jesus from the dead dwells in you, he
who raised Christ Jesus from the dead will give life to
your mortal bodies also through his Spirit which dwells

in you' Rom 8:11)? It seems likely that the Holy Spirit is meant, but that the hymn is much less anxious to make the distinction than modern scholars are.

There is a minor puzzle about when the angels saw Christ; was it at his birth, Lk 2:13–14, or during his lifetime, Mk 1:13, or at his exaltation, pictured as a successful general's victory procession with the (hostile) angelic powers marched along in it in Col 2:15? Given the connection with vindication in the Spirit, this last is the most likely; no doubt there were angelic powers that had fought on God's side and rejoiced in the victory of his Christ, Rev 5:11–12. This victory of Christ is now proclaimed (RSV 'preached'; in fact 'shouted out by a town crier') among the gentiles; this is a basic theme of early christian apocalyptic, as may be seen from the placing of Mk 13:10 in the apocalyptic discourse: 'the gospel must first be preached to all nations.' The immediate object and consequence of preaching is faith, Rom 10:17, so Christ preached among the nations is believed in in the world, though now taken up into the divine glory.

1. 'Who is Christ really, for us today?' What would be your answer to Bonhoeffer's question?

2. The mystery manifested in flesh is clearly the Christ of the church's faith; how important do you think it is to try and get back behind the church's confession to Jesus as he was in his lifetime?

3

False teachers, and pastoral practice
1 Tim 4:1–6:2

1 Tim 4:1–10. Fakirs, mythologers and christians

'Paul'—the writer of the pastorals—was at odds with a group of christian spirituals who seem to have backed up a severe ascetical practice with doctrines—'myths'—about the evil nature of the material creation, or of some part of it. The natural home of such doctrines seems always to have been in southern Asia, at least as far back as Zarathustra in the seventh century BC and his doctrine of the two opposed Gods, the God of light and goodness and the God of darkness and evil. It is a matter of debate among scholars whether this Persian teaching directly affected Greek or Jewish philosophical and religious speculation. The Jewish monastic community at Qumran overlooking the Dead Sea, destroyed in AD 68 and discovered in 1947, has left us a collection of documents containing teachings that may well have been influenced by Persian doctrines. They certainly teach the existence of two opposing spirits of good and evil, and of two whole worlds of good and evil angelic spirits fighting for rule over the world of men. It seems likely that the false teachers that 'Paul' is writing against carried their speculations still further into mythology: the phrase 'godless and silly myths' would not constitute a fair summary of Qumran teaching. And marriage was not forbidden by Qumran, even though some of its members were religious celibates. The false teachers under attack here are, for all their Jewish connections, more dualistic and more doctrinaire.

The author of the pastorals takes the emergence of the false teachers to be a sign that the 'later' or 'last' times prophesied have now come. A comparison with 2 Thes 2:9–12 will show how much of the sharpness of eschatological expectation has gone out of this traditional theme: the doctrines of demons are likely to be around for a good time yet. And, granted his valuation of heterodox christian teaching, 'Paul' was quite correct there. His description of the teachers as 'liars whose consciences are seared' is rather less than helpful; a reasoned critique of their theories would be more to the point. His positive counter-assertions are based upon the fundamental teachings of both OT and NT concerning the material world: God created all of it and it is all good, and may therefore be used and taken with thanksgiving. Thanksgiving is the basic attitude and the basic prayer of man before God in biblical tradition. It is entirely possible that 'Paul' here regards a prayer of thanksgiving over God's creatures as an echo of God's own word concerning his creatures in the first creation story where again and again 'God saw that it was good'.

If Timothy carries out his task of teaching and correcting responsibly he will show himself to be a good minister of Christ Jesus, 4:6. The word there for 'minister' is literally 'deacon', as we noted at 3:8. Even an apostolic delegate, in fact or fiction, like Timothy, was a minister not a hierarch (high priest). 'Ministry' is much the older word for what has, since the time of the later church fathers, been called the hierarchy. Discussion of the absence of the word or notion of priesthood in the pastorals may be postponed till we come to 4:14. The emphasis upon teaching, upon faith in the sense of the object of faith (4:1), and upon what has been entrusted (6:20; 2 Tim 1:12, 14), in the pastorals has sometimes been interpreted too intellectually, too statically, in that sense too objectively. But here Timothy is nourished on the words of the faith, he is a follower, a disciple, of the good teaching. The echo of the theme of discipleship from the gospel is unmistakable; the subject of christian teaching is a person to be followed: Christ Jesus.

St Paul had been fond of sporting metaphors: 'Do you not know that in a race all the runners compete, but only one receives the prize? So run that you may obtain it. Every athlete exercises self-control in all things. They do it to receive a perishable wreath', 1 Cor 9:24ff. Paul's imagery is more vivid and colourful; it is entirely possible that 1 Timothy quotes from a general, proverbial saying: 'While bodily training is of some value, godliness is of value in every way.' To this (possible) proverb a christian conclusion has been added: 'as it holds promise for the present life and also for the life to come.' This turns the pagan proverb into a sure christian saying, one of the collection we met with at 1:15; like most of the others it expresses a relationship between christian life in the present and the hope of life from God in the future. God has life in himself and is the source of all life in others; even death is not the end of everything, for God rescues us from it—'especially . . . those who believe'. There is an endearing vagueness and generous optimism about that last phrase; with all the stress on religion in the pastorals, God retains his mysterious sovereignty, and perhaps he will save even the irreligious and unbelieving.

1. Lecturers in comparative religion still come up with the claim that belief in a god of evil alongside the god of goodness is superior to christian belief; what do you think of that?

2. Is there anything we can usefully learn from the religious myths of other peoples?

3. Asceticism means literally 'athletic exercise'; do you think there is a place for asceticism in the world today?

1 Tim 4:11–16. Timothy and his work

This passage, with its mention of Timothy's youth, has often been claimed as positive proof of the authenticity of the pastorals. A closer look will show that the passage speaks in quite general terms of the duties and the ordination of presbyters save for this one personal reference to Timothy's youth. There may have been a tradition that Timothy was still fairly young when he was put in charge of the congregation at Ephesus. On the other hand it is possible that this passage is in imitation of 1 Cor 16:10: 'When Timothy comes, see that you put him at ease among you, for he is doing the work of the Lord, as I am. So let no one despise him. Speed him on his way in peace, that he may return to me; for I am expecting him with the brethren', and the mention of Timothy's youth is an attempt to explain why people might have despised him. Timothy was younger than Paul in all probability, though we are not directly told so elsewhere, and 'Timothy, my beloved and faithful child in the Lord' in 1 Cor 4:17 (cf Phil 2:22) probably means that Timothy is one of Paul's converts; Paul has just called the Corinthians his beloved children and told them that he became their father in Christ Jesus through the gospel. It is unlikely that there were no middle-aged and old people in the

church at Corinth! Timothy could have been Paul's own
age. Even if he was younger, there is no evidence that he
was a child missionary in the other letters of St Paul or in
the Acts. Something like twelve years are reckoned to
have passed between Ac 16:1ff, when Paul took Timothy
as a helper, and the enigmatic end of Paul's imprisonment
in Rome spoken of at Ac 28:30. (Was Paul martyred then,
as many scholars believe?) The journeys referred to in the
pastorals would have taken a few years more. Though it
might have been possible still to call Timothy a young
man, and to the Greeks men in their thirties could still
be called young men, it is distinctly odd to have people
despising him for his youth after perhaps eighteen years
of missionary work with St Paul.

The two basic tasks of the ministry that are emphasised
once again in this passage are leading and teaching.
Leadership involves setting an example, as it had for
Paul himself: 'Be imitators of me, as I am of Christ', 1 Cor
11:1 (cf 1 Cor 4:16; Phil 3:17). This must be shown in
word and action, embodying the basic christian qualities
of love, faithfulness and purity. Timothy is warned
against youthful passions at 2 Tim 2:22, but in this context 'purity' probably has an even wider reference. Paul is
pictured as retaining the final say over the ministry of the
word at Ephesus, which consists in reading, exhortation
and teaching. These are elements which go back to the
synagogue liturgy. As there, reading would certainly have
meant public reading of the OT in Greek; whether it
would also have included NT readings, and in particular
reading of Paul's epistles, is a matter of conjecture and
depends to some extent on where you place the pastorals
historically. Paul's letters were certainly read out in the
congregations, from his first onwards, 1 Thes 5:27; but
were they regarded as scripture in the church at Ephesus

at this time? Paul's letters are compared with other scriptures at 2 Pet 3:15–16, a letter which may well be the last
of the NT writings. If the pastorals are placed a generation
after St Paul's death then it is very possible that at that
time Paul's letters were read as scripture.

Timothy's 'gift' of 4:14 is clearly an endowment of
the Spirit at the time of his ordination, in which men of
the Spirit took some part. Prophets and speakers in
tongues are said to give thanks, literally 'make eucharist',
at 1 Cor 14:16ff, and that may well include taking part
in the eucharistic prayer itself. It is probable that
prophets took part not only in the selection of candidates
for the presbyterate but also in the prayers that went to
make up the ordination ceremony. The *Didache,* fore-
runner of the later church orders and dating perhaps
from the end of the first century, prescribes the ordination of bishops and deacons who will carry out the work
(the word is 'liturgy' which has both a ritual and a
secular meaning) of the prophets and teachers. We should
not make too rigid a distinction between prophets and
church officers, nor between 'gift' and office. In 1 Cor
12:28–31 apostles, prophets, teachers and administrators
are all listed among those with a special appointment and
gift in the church.

At 2 Tim 1:6 Timothy's gift is said to have been communicated to him through the laying on of Paul's hands.
Here we have a phrase that may be translated either as
'with the laying on of hands for the presbyterate', or as
'when the elders laid their hands on you', RSV. The
abstract noun 'presbyterate' may also be used as a collec-
tive, it may refer either to the office or to the officers. If it
refers to the office, then 2 Tim 1:6 may refer to an
ordination at the hands of Paul acting alone, and 1 Tim
5:22 to Timothy acting in his turn as sole minister of

ordination, and a fancied contradiction resolved. On the other hand, 'the laying on of hands for the presbyterate' does not exclude the participation of the presbyters, nor do 1 Tim 5:22 or 2 Tim 1:6. The question is open.

A scruple may be felt at the thought of Timothy 'saving' himself and others through his leadership and teaching; but in Rom 11:14 Paul had expressed his hope of being able to save his fellow Jews by provoking them to jealousy of the gentiles by his preaching. There is less missionary emphasis in the pastorals, but there is no question about the primacy of grace.

1. Theologians have been speaking of 'the burden of the sacred' felt by priests today; the NT certainly speaks of a burden of care and leadership. How far, do you think, should a burden of good example be laid on the clergy?

2. What form should the ministry of the word take? Could drama and song sometimes replace reading? a discussion session the sermon?

3. Do the more obvious gifts of the Spirit, speaking with tongues and so on, have a part to play in the ministry? Could the possession of pentecostal gifts be part of the qualifications for some clergy?

1 Tim 5:1–16. Relationships with young and old; widows

The first two verses of this chapter are concerned with Timothy's attitude to old and young, men and women; then we go on to consider various groups within the community, widows, 5:3–16, presbyters, 5:17–22, slaves, 6:1–2. Moral teaching and exhortation addressed to different groups within society was a common-place in pagan moral teaching of the time; St Paul had already adapted this to christian use (see, for example, Col 3:18–4:1). Even the direction to treat older men (the same word as the elders, presbyters, of 5:17, but it does not refer specifically here to church officers) as fathers, younger men as brothers and so on can be paralleled in Plato with reference to the guardians of his republic.

Care for (orphans and) widows and a special sensitivity to injustice towards them are strongly marked in the OT (Ex 22:22; Is 1:17). The honouring of parents always included a realistic, pecuniary basis, as the discussion of the commandment in Mk 7:9–13 shows. Honouring of parents was traditionally extended to the 'parents', the old people, of the community as a whole, and especially to the widows who might be without male protection in a patriarchal society. This was institutionalised in the form of an order of widows in the patristic church; we can see the beginnings of this in Ac 6:1 and 9:39. Not all widows belonged to the order; 5:3–8 here refers to widows generally, 5:9–15 to those who belong or must be excluded from the order, 5:16 returns again to widows in general.

The word 'widow' in Greek is connected with words for need, deprivation, and so a 'real widow' is a needy one. Widows with family should not be needy; those that are real widows will take refuge in God, like Anna in Lk 2:36–38. The supplications and prayers of these christian widows will clearly include the public prayers of the church; and to these, no doubt, members of the order of widows would have been specially devoted. But not all 'real widows' would necessarily have reached the age of sixty, and even if, as some scholars have very reasonably suggested, the church was itself concerned in arranging marriage for younger widows (5:11), that was a process that must have taken time, during which some young widows would have been in need of support. Failure to support one's relatives reduces one below the status of unbelievers. St Paul was quite ready to use a like comparison in order to shame the Corinthian christians, 1 Cor 5:1; in the context here the contrast between inside and outside has an extra touch of the christian ghetto about it.

The institution of the order of widows reveals a curious and splendid mixture of idealism and realism. The Lord Christ has not come (whether you place the pastorals at the end of Paul's life or a generation later) and so the eschatological urgency and idealism of 1 Cor 7 *has* to give somewhere: the resolution here embraced is less heroic than that of Paul and of the future orders of women ascetics, in their differing ways. St Paul summoned the widows and virgins in Corinth to total sexual renunciation, while acknowledging perfect christian freedom at all times (1 Cor 7:36); later church practice abandoned the new sixty-year rule *and* dropped the Pauline ruling for freedom. This decision would carry with it unknown consequences for sexual morality, for women and men both. 'When they grow wanton against Christ they desire to marry' is very probably impossible language for the Paul of 1 Corinthians, as I believe for Paul at any time; it is most certainly language that prepares the whole sacral future of the unmarried state in the church. There is no suggestion in 1 Corinthians of virgins and widows being joined to Christ in spiritual marriage; it is probable that Christ is pictured here as the spiritual bridegroom. Marriage to a god, and sacred sexual union in which the earthly representatives, kings and queens, priests and priestesses, became the divine beings they represented in the *hieros gamos* were customary practices in the Mediterranean world of this time. Pagan religious ideas certainly affected the development of christian ideas about celibacy and virginity, to the detriment of christian liberty; 1 Timothy guards against that by the sixty-year rule.

It looks as if there was a kind of noviciate period for candidates for the order of widows, during which they were introduced to the work of the order: caring for children, showing hospitality on behalf of the community, washing the feet of visiting christians, including travelling prophets, and relieving the afflicted. No doubt they were expected to attend faithfully at times of community prayer, as in 5:5, and were expected to be specially devoted to private prayer.

The picture drawn of the behaviour of young widows is lively, if disapproving. It is possible that 'busybodies, saying what they should not' conceals a reference to dabbling in white magic. The word for 'busybodies' is also used in the neuter, as in Ac 19:19, for magic arts; possibly some of the younger members of the order had been dabbling in them on their sick calls. False teachers are probably accused of the same thing in 2 Tim 3:1–9, where the folly of Jannes and Jambres lay in their being Egyptian magicians who tried to best Moses at wonder-working.

There has been some discussion over the identity of the enemy who reviled the christian community over the behaviour of the young widows. In the next verse they are said to have strayed after Satan; Satan is probably meant in 5:14 also, though no doubt he made use of human agents for his reviling!

1. We (the church) have given young women freedom to undertake christian virginity and enter religious orders; do we give them the same freedom to come out again? What about religious brothers? religious priests? priests?

2. *Does the church do enough through religious orders and otherwise to care for orphans, the afflicted, the poor?*

3. *How do parishes nowadays measure up to the duty of hospitality towards visitors? strangers moving into the parish, perhaps from foreign countries? white and black?*

1 Tim 5:17–25. Presbyters

A presbyter is simply an older man, so far as the root meaning of the word goes, and it is used in that sense, as we have seen, at 5:1. The RSV uses 'elder' throughout, which has the advantage of being English; on the other hand, it is only in some christian communities that 'elder' is a title of office and honour in our culture. But in the ancient world, Jewish and Greek, authority was exercised in local and sometimes wider communities by a 'senate', ie a council of elders. 'Presbyter' has the advantage of pointing to the existence of the office, and to the greater honour paid to the old in the hellenistic world. It is also the root from which our English word 'priest' comes, and 'presbyter' may remind us that he was originally thought of primarily as a leader, not as a sacral officer.

We have seen in relation to 3:1 that the church of the pastorals probably had one office of bishop-elder, rather than the Ignatian pattern of the monarchical bishop assisted by a council of elders. 5:17 here opens up the possibility that only some elders exercised leadership, and that only some of those worked in the ministry of the word: the pattern might then have been that of a council including a smaller executive group from which again the liturgical officers were chosen. The 'double honour', involving double pay as 5:18 shows, is puzzling. Did non-

executive elders receive single pay? Why, then, do those
executive leaders who also work hard at the word and
teaching not get triple pay? If the stipend is meant to be
enough to live on why should anyone need double? Paul
always prided himself on being self-supporting, 1 Cor
9:3–18; but he energetically affirmed the right of church
workers to a livelihood from the church, and was the first
to apply the text of Deuteronomy, about not muzzling
oxen during threshing, to this situation, 1 Cor 9:9. The
second quotation given here is more interesting. St Paul
attributes a saying to Jesus that is the same in meaning:
'the Lord commanded that those who proclaim the gospel
should get their living by the gospel', 1 Cor 9:14. The
saying here: 'The labourer deserves his wages' is word
for word a Jesus saying found at Lk 10:7. Of course the
words of the Lord Jesus had equal, if not greater,
authority for Paul as the words of scripture. Here a saying
is quoted precisely as scripture. There are a number of
similarities between the pastorals and Luke–Acts that
have led some scholars to suggest that they are by the same
author, or that Luke acted as Paul's secretary; it is quite
possible that Luke's gospel was read as scripture in the
church of the pastorals. We have already seen that Paul's
letters may have been so read, with reference to 4:13.

The rules for dealing with accusations against elders,
leading on to a ruling against over-hasty ordination, seem
to reflect a history of difficulty in these matters, whether
at Ephesus or elsewhere. Paul's letters show that the
Corinthian christians were a lively and litigious lot, ready
to take one another even before pagan law-courts, 1 Cor
6:1, and Paul provides for the holding of a church court
to take the case of incest dealt with in 1 Cor 5:1–5. He is
of course familiar with the rule from the OT, Deut 19:15;
17:6, that a charge must be supported by two or three

witnesses. When Paul refers to it he does so in his charac-
teristically free manner, applying it to his own repeated
visits to Corinth. No Jewish court would have permitted
a witness to multiply himself by repeated appearances!
The same rule is quoted here in strict legal fashion, as in
Mt 18:16, which is also dealing with church courts. No
doubt 5:20 refers especially to elders, but RSV has introduced 'persist in' into a simple present tense: 'those who
sin'. The RSV version would be in keeping with the rules
given in Mt 18, but it is uncertain that it does not force
the meaning. Judgement given in church courts is a kind
of rehearsal for the last judgement, Mt 18:18; 1 Cor 5:4;
hence it is given in the presence of God and of Christ
Jesus and of the elect angels.

It has been argued that the laying on of hands of 5:22
refers to a gesture of healing and reception back into the
church after a period of exclusion by court judgement.
But we do not know that the penitential and excommunication discipline was so developed even a generation after
St Paul. It is more likely that 'Paul' still has elders in
mind, and is referring to ordination. Careless selection
and ordination would involve moral responsibility for
what followed, if things went wrong. Timothy is to avoid
that.

The word 'pure' (*hagnos*) comes from a root meaning
'holy', but is used to refer to virgins, to those free from
blood-guilt and so on. The slightly puzzling phrase that
follows probably comes in through an association of
ideas. The false teachers forbade the use of foods given
by God, 4:3, and very likely the use of wine also. That
is a superstitious understanding of what christian purity
involves. This verse has given rise to some speculation
about the state of Timothy's digestion, and been claimed
as sure proof of authenticity; was there a tradition at

Ephesus that Paul's co-worker had been sickly? With 5:24-25 we return to the theme of sin in the community, and probably the reference is to elders in particular. The passage ends with the more cheerful observation that there may be a hidden goodness in elders that God will reveal at the proper time.

1. Do you think worker-priests a good idea?

2. Do we worry too much about financial support for church establishments?

3. Do the good effects of the use of alcohol outweigh the bad?

1 Tim 6:1-2. Slaves

The last group within the community to be given moral advice are the slaves. It is true that something will be said about the rich in 6:17-19, but that is by way of appendix to the passage about the false teachers who get caught up with money, 6:5-10. It is notable both here and in Tit 2:9-10 that advice to slaves is not accompanied by advice to masters, as it is in Col 3:22-4:1 and Eph 6:5-9. It is perhaps in keeping with the general emphasis and care for authority in the pastorals.

Slaves were an important element in the early church; Philemon is proof of that, but there are references to them also in 1 Cor 12:13; 1 Cor 7:21-22; Gal 3:28; Col 3:11 among the Paulines, while the members of Caesar's household of Phil 4:22 would be mostly slaves and ex-slaves. Cultivated pagans in Origen's time (third century) mocked the church for being a rabble of slaves and uneducated persons. The early church has often been denounced for not having condemned the institution. At the time when he wrote 1 Corinthians Paul's expectation of the imminent coming of Christ was so urgent as to leave no time for changing the world's institutions, perhaps not even for improving one's own status, if the translation in the RSV footnote to 7:21 is correct: 'Were you a slave when called? Never mind. But if you can gain your freedom, make use of your present condition instead.' A generation after Paul's death the delay in the coming was felt more and more, but it was not till political power came into christian hands that any attempt to change political structures directly was attempted, and even then it has been claimed that the Constantinian Roman empire transformed the church more than the church the empire: a false claim containing much truth. At the time that the pastorals were written a church containing many slaves and poor people was not in a position to work for freedom directly; direct non-violent action for political purposes was not thought of, violent rebellion was not the business of christians as such, and would inevitably have led to the same terrible end as the slaves' revolt under Spartacus, still remembered after nearly two hundred years.

The advice to slaves given here, therefore, depends upon an acceptance of the institution. Masters have a real right to respect from their slaves, so that christian teaching would rightly be spoken ill of if it encouraged slaves to disobedience. The pastorals are very sensitive about the church's good name, though anticipations of this may be found in the certain Paulines, 1 Thes 4:10–12. If pagan masters have a right to respect, christian ones have a right to more. This implies that christian slaves are benefactors to their brothers and masters; the word 'service' is used of public service to the state, literally 'well-doing'.

1. *What do you think the church should have done about slavery?*

2. *Does christian 'other-worldliness' necessarily support evil structures and institutions?*

4

Conclusion to 1 Timothy
1 Tim 6:3–21

1 Tim 6:2d–10. False teaching and money

In the circling, repetitive movement of the letter we return to the theme of true and false teaching. The true teaching is, of course, that which accords with religion; the first phrase is more telling: 'the sound words of our Lord Jesus Christ'. They probably mean that the Lord Jesus is not only the central theme of church teaching, but also its source and guarantor, even where explicit reference is not made to the tradition of the Jesus sayings as found in the gospels.

The false teachers are denounced in spirited fashion for vanity, superficiality and quarrelsomeness, but we do not learn anything here of the content of their teaching. The one new feature is the accusation of venality and greed for money. This is contrasted with the true christian spirit of religious frugality. 'Contentment' is a word with stoic overtones, found already in Phil 4:11 as an adjective: 'I have learned, in whatever state I am, to be content.' The phrases which follow about men carrying nothing into or out of this world are found in the Greek moralists also, but are equally to be found in the OT: 'As he came from his mother's womb he shall go again, naked as he came, and shall take nothing for his toil, which he may carry away in his hand', Eccl 5:15. Very likely both these sources are in the author's mind, but above all, in the light of the reference to the Lord Jesus' teaching, the celebrated passage on the birds of the air in the sermon on the mount, Mt 6:25–33.

The contrasting verses on the rich still have the false teachers particularly in mind, as the phrase about wandering away from the faith shows, 6:10; but what is said has a wider application, looking forward to the lines on the rich in 6:17. 6:10a, 'for the love of money is (a) root of all evils', is a proverb current in both Greek and Latin; popular in the middle ages, as Chaucer shows, it is worth noting in a time when some marxists are christians that the proverb seems to regard avarice as a partial, though universal, cause of human woes.

1. How far can we regard the Lord Jesus as the guarantor of christian teaching, and especially christian moral teaching?

2. Is argumentativeness a note of heretical theology?

3. Is the love of money a note of heretical theology?

1 Tim 6:11–16. Living for God

This passage of exhortation will apply in the first place to Timothy in a letter apparently addressed to him; given the stress laid upon community officers, 'man of God' will refer more particularly to the presbyters. It is a phrase used of Moses, Deut 33:1, of David, Neh 12:24, but above all of prophets, eg 1 Sam 2:27. But at 1 Tim 2:8 all christian men stand lifting holy hands in prayer for all men, after the fashion of Moses on the hill-top praying for Israel, Ex 17:12. We are told in 2 Tim 3:16–17 that all scripture is inspired and profitable for training, that the 'man of God' may be equipped for every good work.

The context is addressed to Timothy personally, but that particular sentence seems to apply to all christians. There is no sufficient reason here either to restrict the meaning to Timothy or to church ministers; there is nothing in this passage that does not apply to all christians.

Christians are to run after righteousness and faith; in Rom 9:30 Paul had praised the gentiles for pursuing righteousness through faith. Godliness, or religion, is the favoured way in the pastorals of referring to christian goodness; faith, love and steadfastness are Paul's own way, I Thes 1:3, and no doubt our 6:11 reflects that verse. 'Fight the good fight' narrows down the Greek metaphor, which refers to any kind of athletic contest; again Paul was fond of metaphors drawn from the Greek games, 1 Cor 9:24ff. The 'good confession' of 6:12 almost certainly refers to baptismal confession; baptism is certainly a call to eternal life, Rom 6:13. The baptismal confession was originally a simple confession that Jesus is Lord, Rom 10:9; 1 Cor 12:3; later a three-fold form came into use, Mt 28:19. Two-clause credal forms are also to be found, 1 Cor 8:6; is 6:13 such a two-clause creed with 'I charge you in the presence' replacing 'I believe in the name'? Jesus' confession should not be taken restrictively to refer to his trial; his witnessing is sealed by his death as a witness, a martyr. Baptismal confession is participation in Jesus' own confession. Baptism and christian life, the pattern (commandment) of which is taken on at baptism, looks forward to the appearing (epiphany) of the Lord at the end of time. God is the one who brings time to an end, and so anticipation of the coming leads into a doxology (praise) of God, an early christian hymn. The image of God dwelling in light inaccessible, whom no man can see, reminds us of the prologue to the fourth gospel, itself dependent upon OT motifs, where God reveals himself in his Word as light, while himself remaining the unseen God, Jn 1:18. 1 Timothy is faithful to the fundamental biblical and NT paradox: God would not be God if he could cease to be the impenetrable mystery at the heart of the world, yet in Christ the fullness of the divine mystery is embodied and disclosed.

1. Should belief in God as the future of man mean anything for christian life here and now?

2. Is it important to cultivate a sense of the mystery and awesomeness of God together with our belief that he is for us in Christ?

3. What does the coming of Christ mean after 2,000 years of apparent not-coming?

1 Tim 6:17–21. Advice to the rich and a farewell to Timothy

The remarks on the rich in 6:7–10 were particularly directed to the false teachers, so a piece of advice is given here to rich people generally. It is an untidy way of writing, and a distinct come-down after the ringing phrases of the doxology.

The rich are rich in this world-age only; it is foolishness to give way to pride on that account. We are reminded of the story of the foolish rich man in Lk 12:16–21. That too ends with a contrast between present riches that we have to leave one day and the abiding riches of God. Wisdom for the rich is to make use of their property in doing good to others, like the steward in the gospel who made friends for himself by means of unrighteous mammon, as an example to those who hope to be received into the eternal habitations, Lk 16:9. Alms-

giving out of trust in God is a good foundation for the
future, in the gospel it means treasure in heaven,
Lk 12:33.

After these few words to the rich, the letter ends with
a final warning to Timothy to avoid false teaching, and
instead to guard the tradition of the church entrusted to
him. (Cf 2 Tim 1:14.) Again we do not learn much
about what the false teachers actually taught, for all that
it was profane chatter and a 'knowledge' that did not
deserve the word. Paul had difficulties with people who
prided themselves on their 'knowledge' that idols are
nothing, and food offered to them simply food, 1 Cor 8.
These false teachers seem to have been misguided about
food, 1 Tim 4:3; their false knowledge separates them
from faith, which is not so much knowing as being known,
1 Cor 8:3.

The letter ends with a greeting identical with that at
the end of Colossians, even to the plural! Clearly, as we
have seen throughout, it is not so much a personal letter
as a letter addressed to a whole church together with its
ministers.

*1. We saw earlier that the church has often been
attacked for condoning slavery; is she not equally guilty
for having 'condoned' possession of riches?*

*2. Can, and should, almsgiving be replaced by letting
people have what it is their right to have?*

*3. Is heresy parasitic upon true tradition; or does the
'deposit of faith' grow by way of reaction to experimental
and often misguided speculations?*

5

The work of the ministry
2 Tim 1:1–2:13

2 Tim 1:1–5. Greeting and prayer

The opening greeting of 2 Timothy is very like that of
1 Timothy, with only minor differences. The greatest
difference is that in 1 Timothy Paul was said to be 'an
apostle . . . by command of . . . Christ Jesus our hope';
here he is 'an apostle . . . according to the promise of the
life which is in Christ Jesus'. Biblical hope is founded
upon God's promise. God's action even in past and
present has imprinted within it a pointer to the future, is
promise in action. So the exaltation of Christ, the supreme
action of God to date, anticipates his coming in glory at
the end. That is why he is our hope, in him God's future
is already coming to fulfilment, the life of God is both
revealed and shared with us, with a view to a fuller sharing in that future. In this way the greeting in 2 Timothy
makes explicit the meaning of the phrase in 1 Timothy.

It was customary in the hellenistic world to go on from
the opening greeting of a letter to a prayer, often a prayer
of thanksgiving to the gods for some favour received.
Paul had christianised this custom, and 2 Timothy follows
suit. It is not entirely clear what 'Paul' gives thanks for
precisely; presumably it is Timothy's 'sincere faith' of
1:5, and 'Paul' is combining prayer with exhortation.

'God whom I serve' could be translated 'whom I worship', as in the corresponding phrase in Rom 1:9. 'To worship with a clear conscience' then links up not only with Rom 1:9: 'I serve with my spirit in the gospel', but with Rom 12:1, and the spiritual worship, which is christian living, with 'worship in Spirit and in truth', Jn 4:24, and with the 'spiritual sacrifices' of 1 Pet 2:5. This is in fact a theme running right through the NT, the replacement of blood sacrifices and temple worship by life and prayer in Christ. The basic theme is given a characteristic twist here in the direction of a moral feeling in danger of complacency—the contrast with 1 Cor 4:3–4 is very marked: 'I do not even judge myself. I am not aware of anything against myself, but I am not thereby acquitted. It is the Lord who judges me.' This phrase of 2 Timothy is more intelligible if the writer is really speaking of the hero-apostle of the past.

Timothy's tears of 1:4 are presumably those he shed on parting from Paul. This seems to suppose a scene like that of Ac 20:36–38, where Paul said farewell to the elders of the church at Ephesus on his journey up to Jerusalem where he anticipated imprisonment and possible death, 20:22–23. 2 Timothy is written as from prison and under sentence of death, 4:6, and has a number of themes in common with Paul's speech in Ac 20: the apostle's faithfulness in life and teaching, Ac 20:18–21; 2 Tim 3:10, his anxiety over false teachers, Ac 20:29–30; 2 Tim 4:3–4 etc, his concern for the succession of leaders and teachers, Ac 20:28; 2 Tim 4:5–6; 2:2. In Ac 20 Paul is still a free man and still has to accomplish his course, 20:24; in 2 Timothy he is enduring his last imprisonment and already, in anticipation, looks back over the race, 4:7 ('course', same word) he has finished ('accomplished', same word). Incidentally, it is probable that Ac 20, and the speeches in Acts generally, are as they stand compositions of 'Luke', though they incorporate much traditional material. The likeness between Ac 20 and 2 Timothy constitutes a very useful clue to the possible method of the writing of the pastorals.

'Paul's' mention of his longing to see Timothy once again anticipates the request of 4:9, 21 that Timothy come to Paul soon, before winter sets in and makes travel impossibly dangerous. There is a definite tension between this request, and the whole passage 4:9–21, and the finality of the valedictory tone in 4:6–8.

In Ac 16:1, when Timothy was first introduced to us, we were told that his mother was a Jewess married to a (pagan) Greek, and that she had become a christian. Now in 2 Timothy we learn that her name was Eunice, and that her mother Lois had become a christian too. These personal details are almost certainly true ones concerning Timothy's family that have come down by tradition to the author of the pastorals.

1. Do we think often enough of God's promise in Christ?

2. How will we find the right balance between thanksgiving and petition in our prayer?

2 Tim 1:6–14. Timothy should imitate Paul

Timothy's mother and grandmother have just been mentioned in the implicit exhortation to Timothy to be strong in faith, which is their faith also. In this passage Timothy is explicitly summoned to a renewal of courage and strength—apparently he has been hesitant in witnessing to Christ, which is his duty in a special way since he is an official teacher in the christian community, ordained by Paul himself for the work. This hint of diffidence and timidity in Timothy is of a piece with that aspect of his character touched on in a rather puzzling way, as we saw, at 1 Tim 4:12: some people in the community found Timothy a lightweight, undeserving of respect.

This suggestion of timidity is the only personal touch in the passage, which focuses on the role of the church minister as successor in the work of the apostle and martyr. We have seen that there is no mention of ordination in the certainly authentic letters of Paul. Whether or not ordination came in after Paul's time in the Pauline churches, as I believe, this passage is an important clue to the meaning of ordination, the laying on of hands. 1 Tim 4:14 spoke of the communication of a gift—of course from God, as this passage explicitly states. This gift is one of a divine Spirit, of power and love, that is like a fire lodged in the spirit of the one ordained, 1:6. The Pentecostal Spirit came in wind and flames of fire, Ac 2:1ff, and Paul commanded the Thessalonians not to 'quench' the fiery Spirit of prophecy, I Thes 5:19. In the light of those passages we will surely be right to see a reference to the Holy Spirit here; it is more difficult, and less interesting, to discover whether his presence and gift is thought to be mediated through a created 'spirit' of ordination. Wind and fire are symbols of the power of the Spirit: it was central to Paul's teaching about the Spirit that the greatest of his gifts is love: 1 Cor 12:31b–13:13; Rom 5:5. Love brings with it a whole scale of God-given qualities, among which self-control finds a place, Gal 5:23. The Greek word for 'self-control' that is added to 'love' here at 2 Tim 1:7 is different—it starts from the notion of keeping a right mind in the midst of passions and desires—but has much the same meaning. It is not easy to decide whether 2 Timothy has slipped into moralising generalities or whether Timothy is being asked to rise above his fears.

From 1:8 Paul the apostle and martyr is held up as an example to the christian minister. Suffering for the sake of the gospel is part of the vocation of every christian, Rom 8:17, and in a special way of apostles and missionaries, 2 Cor 4:7–12. Imprisonment in defence of the gospel is to be accounted a grace, a grace in which ordinary christians take their share along with Paul, Phil 1:7ff. Here in 2 Timothy a special emphasis is laid upon Timothy as representative of those who stand in the succession of the apostle's work for the gospel.

The gospel is now briefly stated in a couple of verses that have a solemn liturgical ring about them; probably this is another echo of an early christian hymn. The hymn was surely composed in a Pauline church; the contrast between works and grace is basic in Paul's theology (Gal 2:16 and frequently); there is a parallel contrast, again in a liturgical-sounding passage, between deeds ('works', the same word) and mercy in Tit 3:5. Grace is the embodiment of God's eternal purpose, and is given from eternity in the pre-existent Christ; cf Eph 1:4, we were chosen in Christ before the foundation of the world. What was once hidden from human eyes in the heavenly Christ has now been revealed in the earthly epiphany of Christ our saviour, 1:10. The root of the Greek word 'epiphany' has already been used at 1 Tim 3:16: Christ the mystery of God has undergone 'epiphany' in the flesh; a similar verb is used of the incarnation of Christ in Tit 3:4: 'when the goodness and loving kindness of God our saviour underwent epiphany'. Elsewhere 'epiphany' is used of Christ's appearance in glory at the end of the world, 2 Tim 4:1, 8.

Christ has already abolished death and brought life and immortality to light. In 1 Cor 15:26 death is the last enemy still to be destroyed; but in v 57 of the same chapter God is already thanked as the one who is giving us victory over death through Christ. Christ is now our life, Col 3:4, he lives to God with unending life, Rom 6:10, his resurrection implies immortality for all mortal men, 1 Cor 15:53, a share in the immortality of God himself, Rom 1:23.

Paul was appointed herald, apostle and teacher of the gospel, as in 1 Tim 2:7. Proclamation is falling into the background in the pastorals, though witness to Christ through suffering has necessarily a missionary character, and is in continuity with the apostle's own proclamation of the gospel at his (last?) trial, 2 Tim 4:17, cf Phil 1:7, 12–14. But the primary emphasis falls upon leadership and teaching, functions dependent upon apostolic appointment, directly in Timothy's case, indirectly in the case of those appointed by Timothy in his turn, 2 Tim 2:2. Apostleship involves suffering, but Paul is not ashamed of the gospel. In Rom 1:16 the reason given is that the gospel is the power of God for salvation; here in 2 Timothy, in keeping with the shift in the generations and the corresponding shift from gospel to the 'pattern of sound words', 1:13, the reason for non-shame is trust in God, the guardian of the trust given to Paul first and then to Timothy, 1:12 and 1:14, the saving truth of Christ that will be fully revealed at the last day. For the present we hold to this truth in faith and love towards God, and the indwelling Spirit guards this good treasure within us, until the day of God comes.

1. Is it possible to drop clerical power and believe in the Spirit's power given to those ordained?

2. Does the movement from ministerial vocation to christian calling in this passage, 1:6, 9, imply that the christian vocation is basic and primary?

3. Does too much preservation deaden the gospel? Can the gospel live without change?

2 Tim 1:15–18. Onesiphorus the faithful

These four verses belong with 4:9–22, and are very probably a fragment from a genuine Pauline letter. Together they point to Paul's arrest at Ephesus, the obvious occasion for those in Asia, the province of which Ephesus was the capital, to turn away from Paul. In contrast to the rest of the christian community Onesiphorus stood by Paul and helped him, and even followed him to Rome to give him what help he could. Onesiphorus seems to have died since, for the mention of his household only here and above all in the greetings in chapter 4 is inexplicable otherwise. The prayer of 1:18 comes in by way of parenthesis, and some scholars who accept the authenticity of these verses have taken the prayer for a later addition. There is no explicit mention of prayer for the dead in Paul's certain letters, though there is a mysterious reference to baptism on behalf of the dead in 1 Cor 15:29, and baptism without prayer would have been an oddity, since sacrifice and prayer for the dead was certainly practised, 2 Mac 12:39–45. And certainly Paul believed that christians will stand in need of God's saving action in Christ on the future day of wrath, Rom 5:9. The prayer asks quite simply that the Lord Christ (?) will grant Onesiphorus mercy from the Lord God (?) on judgement day.

1. Does the church do enough for people in prison?
2. Does prayer for the dead have a place in your personal life? Should it have one?

2 Tim 2:1–7. The succession, and support, of ministers

The grace that is in Christ Jesus seems to refer primarily to the fundamental gift of God given to every christian, which underlies and empowers the specific grace given to ministers, 1:6. 2:2 may possibly refer back in similar fashion to baptism, which was from the first associated with instruction in faith and confession of faith, Rom 10: 5–17. The second half of the verse certainly goes on to speak of the instruction of others in turn as teachers, which would, in the context of the pastorals, imply ordination; it is even possible that it looks forward to a further generation of ministers: the faithful men teach others and among those others must be included these further ministers. Behind this whole succession stands the authority of the apostle. Such at least is the claim made by the letter, and even if the historical derivation of the ministry was in fact more complex—was there an intermediate stage of travelling prophets between the apostles and the fully established presbyter-bishops, as the *Didache* suggests?—the claim is surely justified theologically. It is a basic element of the sacramental principle that the necessary and all-powerful grace of God comes to us through the contingencies and fragilities of human history.

Timothy is now exhorted once again to endure his share of apostolic suffering, cf 1:8, like a soldier in war. Paul was fond of military metaphors, from his first letter onwards, 1 Thes 5:8; here it is developed further to bring out the theme of single-minded devotion to duty. The soldiering metaphor suggests two others: one from the games, another favourite with Paul, 1 Cor 9:24, where the religious duty of observing the rules of training stands for the 'rules' of the ministry; one from farming which occurs in much the same form in 1 Cor 9:10, where the point is the material support of the minister. 1 Cor 9:9, the typological application of Deut 25:4, has already been echoed to make the same point at 1 Tim 5:18. Clearly the proper support of pastors was something of a problem in the church of the pastorals.

1. Should apostolic succession stand or fall by direct and fully explicit ordination, by apostles, of pleni-potentiary successors?

2. Has the church militant sometimes taken the military metaphor too literally? How should we come to terms with the blood-stained history of christendom?

2 Tim 2:8–13. Salvation through suffering

The fundamental reason for the inevitable suffering of apostolic men is that such is part of christian existence, founded upon the life and mystery of Christ himself. So the epistle takes up this basic theme of the gospel. The wording is reminiscent once again of the Pauline letters. 'Jesus Christ, risen from the dead, descended from David' is an echo, in inverted order, of Rom 1:3–4, itself, as we have seen, an echo of an early christian creed. The apostle's suffering is a participation in Christ's suffering, endured for the sake of others, cf Col 1:24; 2 Cor 1:5–6. Suffering is effective on behalf of the elect; but we should not interpret this passage too restrictively; God desires the salvation of all, and Christ gave himself as a ransom for all, 1 Tim 2:4–5.

The sure saying that follows is in rhythmic balanced form, an early christian hymn, possibly from a baptismal liturgy. Again the words and ideas are reminiscent of

Paul; dying with Christ in hope of life with him is the
theme of, eg, 2 Cor 4:8–11. To sit in judgement upon
the world and angels, 1 Cor 6:2–3, implies reigning with
Christ; that was explicitly promised to the twelve in
Mt 19:28, as a participation in the glory of the heavenly
Davidic messiah. That denial of Christ here on earth involves denial by Christ on judgement day is stated in
Mt 10:33. But this cannot mean that Christ denies himself and the truth of God; he is God's 'yes' addressed to
creation in final trustworthiness, 2 Cor 1:19. And so,
unexpectedly, even when we are faithless, he remains
faithful.

*1. If God's word cannot be fettered, why do we need to
compromise with the powers of this world? What price
concordats?*

*2. Is Christ God's 'yes' only as saviour, or already as the
incarnation of God? What difference would this make to
our picture of the world?*

6
False teaching
2 Tim 2:14–4:22

2 Tim 2:14–26. False teaching and controversy

2 Timothy now turns to the constant preoccupation of the pastorals: false teaching. Once again there is no attempt at refutation: the false teachings are simply rejected out of hand as incompatible with the truth of christian faith handed down by tradition. False teachings are simply disputes about words, 2:14, stupid, senseless controversies that only breed quarrels, 2:23, godless chatter leading to further ungodliness, 2:16. The only scrap of information about its real nature is that it was claimed that the resurrection is past already, 2:18. Already in 1 Cor 15 Paul had had to struggle with christian unbelief in the resurrection which he did by constructing a great theological argument to establish the truth and centrality of the resurrection. The error here in 2 Timothy seems to consist in an inadmissible spiritualisation ('demythologisation' if you like) of the resurrection: present christian participation in the new life of Christ from God is taken to be the true meaning of the resurrection.

Two of the false teachers are named, Hymenaeus and Philetus; Hymenaeus has already been mentioned in 1 Tim 1:20. To their false teaching there stands in opposition and refutation God's firm foundation; this is surely the church. A related metaphor is found at 1 Tim 3:15, where the church is the pillar and bulwark of truth, resting ultimately upon the foundation of Christ and God. The foundation bears two inscriptions that exclude the false teachers: the first shows that they do not belong to the Lord, the second is a warning to faithful christians to avoid them. There is a new foundation-stone prophesied for Jerusalem in Is 28:16, bearing the legend: 'He who believes will not be in haste'.

This mention of the foundation leads on to a muddled metaphor of the church as a great house full of vessels, noble and ignoble. Paul had made a similar comparison in terms of vessels for beauty and for menial use, vessels of mercy and vessels of destruction, Rom 9:21–23. But 2 Timothy, by bringing both types of vessel within the one house, reminds us inevitably of the parable of the noble and ignoble members of the body, which is the church, cf 1 Cor 12:12–26, where both are good and useful. Then the noble vessels are commanded to purify themselves from the ignoble ones—a very odd conception.

The real point is brought out in what follows. The language is very general, and is surely intended not only for christian ministers but also, for the most part, christians simply. They are to shun youthful passions, where presumably sexual ones are particularly in mind, and seek after the basic qualities of christian existence, righteousness, faith, love and peace, along with their faithful fellow-christians, cf 1 Cor 1:2. A similar list is given at 1 Tim 6:11; God's servant must avoid quarrels and teach in a sensible way—here the ministers of the church are meant, and correction is one of their functions, 1 Tim 5:20. The ultimate purpose of correction and court process in the church is that the guilty may repent, and be delivered from the devil to whom, in accordance with the rule of corresponding punishment (*lex talionis*), they had been handed over by the church, 1 Cor 5:5.

1. Is a 'spiritual' interpretation of the resurrection necessary or desirable in our times?

2. Is to shun them the best thing we can do with human passions?

3. Do you think the devil is at work in the church and the world today?

2 Tim 3:1–9. False teaching and eschatological happening

This passage hints that the false teachers dabbled in magic, 3:8–9, and puts their folly against a lurid background of the eschatological paroxysm of sin in this world. The list of sins in 3:2–5 includes an accusation of excessive love of money that we have met with in 1 Tim 6:5–10, and will again at Tit 1:11. Otherwise the list is sweeping in scope, similar to other general lists found in the hellenistic moral philosophers, and curiously like the one describing pagan depravity in Rom 1:29–31. The most puzzling item is the last: 'holding the form of religion but denying the power of it', since the false teaching seems to include an element of superstition, an excessive affirmation of religious power. The point probably is that true religion, the disciplined, traditional christianity of the pastorals, is not enough for these followers of Jannes and Jambres. These are the names given in late Jewish tradition to the Egyptian magicians who opposed Moses in ancient times, cf Ex 7:11. It seems that these new practitioners of magic had particular success among christian women. It looks rather as if the phrases 'weak women, burdened with sins and swayed by various impulses' betray 'Paul's' attitude to women generally, rather than indicating a particular group of women, cf 1 Tim 2:9–15. It is worth remembering, in contrast, the praise of Lois and Eunice in 1:5 and the inclusion of Prisca and Claudia in the roll of honour in 4:19–21. But in any case the success of these latter-day magicians will be short-lived, like that of Jannes and Jambres themselves.

1. Do you expect this wicked world-age to end with a bang or a whimper, or neither?

2. Do you think women are more tempted by magic and superstition than men?

3. Should our attitude to magic and superstition be one of simple opposition and enmity?

2 Tim 3:10–17. Timothy is to follow the apostle's example

The calm, almost placid, description of Paul's apostolic life, work and sufferings is very different in tone from that given in 2 Cor 11:16–12:13; there is an impersonal note of tradition about it. The geographical reference to Antioch, Iconium and Lystra is unexpected also; many of the more spectacular sufferings listed in 2 Corinthians would not have taken place there, and yet the real Timothy is likely to have stood nearer to many of these later sufferings. The reference is intelligible on the part of an historian who knew both that Timothy came from Lystra, Ac 16:1–2, and that Paul had had to suffer on his first visit to those regions, Ac 13:50, 14:5, 19. Each reader will make up his own mind on the question.

The contrast between faithful christians and deceivers, 3:12–13, obviously includes a contrast between true and false teachers. There may be another hint at the magical practices of the false teachers; 'impostors' could equally be translated as 'witches'.

Timothy is next commanded to be faithful to the tradition and the scriptures of God. The phrases 'knowing from whom you learned it' and 'how from childhood you have been acquainted' point unmistakably to Timothy; but the passage as a whole, and particularly the description and praise of scripture, are clearly universal in scope. It is to be noted that tradition is described in the language of discipleship and faith; faith and tradition, discipleship and God's word, belong inexorably together.

Scripture is said, all of it, to be 'inspired-by-God'. This word occurs only here in the NT, but the idea is a traditional Jewish one, and is closely paralleled in the statement about the prophets in 1 Pet 1:10–12. For a full understanding of that passage we have to remember that in Jewish tradition the law is even holier than the prophets, and that the prophets included many books we list among the historicals. Psalms were inspired by the Holy Spirit also, cf Mk 12:36.

As inspired, the scriptures are basic for christian teaching and education—'training' here is the Greek word for education—which will include correction and rebuke. Only so may the christian, the man of God, be fully equipped for all the demands of christian life.

1. Should imitation of the saints be part of our understanding of membership of the church?

2. Are good christians, or for that matter good people, more subject to trouble than anyone else? Should they be?

3. What is the right relationship between scripture and tradition?

2 Tim 4:1–8. 'Paul's' last testament to Timothy

As the letter moves towards its conclusion, a noble passage of farewell is placed before the end instructions and greetings. The farewell echoes a number of themes from Paul's own letters, and is reminiscent besides of Ac 20. The farewell is absolutely final in tone, the instructions and greetings are perfectly open-ended. It is easy to imagine someone creating 4:1–8 by way of imaginative construction, as the author of Ac 20 has done; 4:9–22 are more likely to be genuine Paul, of interest only because they concern him.

The farewell is liturgical in style at beginning and end, with the solemn evocations of the day of judgement. Behind the evocation of the eschatological witnesses, God and Christ, epiphany and kingdom, of 4:1 stands the OT liturgical and juridical style, where appeal is made to the cosmic witnesses, eg Is 1:2: 'Hear, O heavens, and give ear, O earth; for the Lord has spoken. . . .' The NT example is naturally stamped with a greater intimacy of approach to Christ and God. That Christ is judge of the living and the dead is a theme that goes back probably to very early christian proclamation, Ac 10:42, and runs through the NT, Mt 25:31–46; 1 Pet 4:5; Jn 8:16.

The duties urged upon Timothy in 4:2 spring from the nature of the gospel itself, which is proclamation, challenge, conviction, rebuke, exhortation and teaching. The continuity with the description of the OT scripture at 3:16 stands out equally.

Now there follows a final word of warning against instability of belief and false teaching mixed up with myths, cf Ac 20:30, 1 Tim 1:4 etc. In contrast Timothy is to be faithful and enduring as the apostle himself in the work of preaching the gospel. ('Evangelist' does not have a technical meaning here, as it has at Ac 21:8, Eph 4:11.)

The mention of libation and departure in 4:6 constitutes a double echo of Philippians, where at 2:17 Paul
looked forward to the possibility of sacrificial martyrdom,
the blood of martyrdom being identified with the red
wine of sacrificial libation, and spoke of his death as a
departure, a casting loose of his ship of death, 1:23. The
two images come together very aptly here in 2 Timothy;
the casting off of a ship at the beginning of a voyage was
the occasion for a libation to the gods in the ancient pagan
world. Behind both passages stands the late Jewish understanding of the death of the martyrs of Israel as sacrifice,
cf 4 Mac 6:28.

Once again the work of apostleship is compared to the
athletes' struggles in the games, cf 2:5; 1 Tim 6:12, and
to the running of a race, 1 Cor 9:24. At the end of the
contest the apostle (and after him the missionary, and indeed every christian) can look forward to crowning with
the victor's wreath, 2 Tim 2:5; 1 Cor 9:25. It is not entirely clear whether 'righteousness' points to the basis of
the struggle, Rom 5:9, or whether it points to ultimate
vindication in God's law-court on the last day. Perhaps
2 Timothy has both in mind; righteousness is certainly
basic to christian life and education, 3:16, while here in
4:8 the 'righteous' judge awards the crown of 'righteousness'. For this same reward all those who look forward in
love to the coming (here 'epiphany') of the Lord Jesus
may hope. Though the time perspectives of the pastorals
have expanded to allow for an indefinite time of the
church, cf 2:2, the eschatological hope of primitive
Pauline christianity remains firm.

*1. Is there a method of distinguishing 'itching ears'
that turn to false novelties from a search for the renewal
of old truths?*

2. *Does the language of libation-sacrifice applied to the death of the apostle throw any light on the character of his priesthood? Cf Phil 2:17, and Rom 15:16.*

2 Tim 4:9–22. Last instructions and greetings

It is only in the context of 2 Timothy that these instructions and greetings appear as the final ones, given in full consciousness of that fact, of the apostle Paul. Taken in themselves they speak of a reprieve from immediate danger, the 'lion's mouth' of 4:17b, and look forward to some months of work; no prediction of what is to happen after that is attempted. These verses are very probably a genuine fragment from St Paul, preserved out of piety rather than from any desire to authenticate the letter as a whole. Their placing here in 2 Timothy points to the likelihood that they do in fact come from Paul's final imprisonment, which tradition places at Rome. They were surely addressed to Timothy, who may or may not have been at Ephesus at the time. 4:12 has been taken to suggest otherwise; if it does, it is not so much because of the mention of Ephesus as if it were a third place extra to Paul's and Timothy's, cf 1 Cor 15:32, as the apparent lack of connection between Tychicus and Timothy. It would be unlike Paul to send Tychicus to Timothy without a word of commendation or an indication of some special gift or usefulness, cf Col 4:7–9. A. T. Hanson has suggested Colossae as a likely place for Timothy to be. The greetings to Prisca and Aquila, and to the household of Onesiphorus, 4:19, point to a nearness to Ephesus; Timothy is to come via Troas, 4:13; Colossae will certainly fit. There is a considerable tension between the summons to Timothy to rejoin Paul and the whole tenor of 1 and 2 Timothy, which place Timothy as resident apostolic delegate at Ephesus, at grips with major problems in the basic teaching of the gospel.

Demas was with Paul (at Rome?) when he wrote to the Colossians from his prison, 4:14, Philem 24. Paul obviously feels that Demas has let him down by going off to Thessalonica; there is no need to suppose that he has apostasised. It is not certain whether Crescens went to Galatia or Gaul, the MS tradition is divided, and Gaul was called 'Galatia' in Greek anyway. He bore a Latin name, and tradition makes him a founder of the church of Vienne. No rebuke is uttered against him; it is likely that it was missionary work that took him away. Similarly, Titus has gone to Dalmatia, to the north of the limit of Paul's own work in the eastern Mediterranean, Nicopolis in Epirus, Rom 15:19 and Tit 3:12. Luke, the beloved physician of Col 4:14 and fellow worker with Paul, Philem 24, is still with Paul.

Timothy is asked to bring Mark with him when he comes. The name is a very common one, but this Mark is surely Barnabas' cousin, Col 4:10, and the companion of Paul and Barnabas on part of their first missionary journey out of Antioch, Ac 13:1–3 and 5; 15:36–39. A reconciliation had obviously been effected before the time Colossians was written, and Mark has made himself useful as a personal assistant to Paul. Tychicus is mentioned by way of parenthesis—see above and Eph 6:21–2—then Paul asks for his thick winter cloak, his books (including a bible—OT—or parts of one?) and his parchments (vellum codices containing Paul's own work and notes?).

Alexander was naturally a very common name; one was mentioned at 1 Tim 1:20, presumably then resident at Ephesus; another, a Jewish spokesman in spite of his name, at Ac 19:33–4, again at Ephesus. There is nothing to indicate any connection with this Alexander, coppersmith and opponent of Paul; nor do we know when he opposed Paul's words, at his arrest (Ephesus?) or at his first defence (at Rome?), or during Paul's preaching before his arrest. Paul's 'first defence' was presumably his preliminary investigation, the *prima actio*, under Roman law, perhaps at Rome at the beginning of his present (second?) imprisonment. Paul, as was his custom, Ac 21:37–22:22; 22:30–23:10; 24:10–25; 25:6–26:32, had been able to turn the case into an opportunity for preaching the gospel and had escaped condemnation (the 'lion's mouth' is a biblical phrase for acute danger, Ps 22:21, not to be taken literally). Paul looks forward to final rescue, in and through martyrdom, or otherwise.

Timothy is asked to greet Prisca and Aquila, known to us from Ac 18:1–3, 18–19, 26; from Rom 16:3, which may have been part of a letter to Ephesus, and from 1 Cor 16:19 where the church in their house at Ephesus is mentioned. They are presumably in Ephesus at this time; Timothy would be expected to pass through it on his way to Troas and Rome.

News is given of Erastus and Trophimus. Erastus is presumably Timothy's old companion and Paul's helper of Ac 19:22; it is not likely that he is Erastus the city treasurer of Rom 16:23 who is likely to have been a more sedentary person. Trophimus, like Timothy and Tychicus, had been bearers of the great collection for Jerusalem on Paul's last (?) journey there, Ac 20:4; on that occasion he had passed safely through Miletus, 20:15, and up to Jerusalem, 21:29. This obviously refers to a different, and presumably later, occasion.

The last three names of 4:21 are Latin ones; a respectable tradition, recorded by Irenaeus, places Linus as first bishop of Rome in succession to Peter. The earlier evidence of 1 Clement and the *Shepherd of Hermas* suggests that the monarchical episcopate was late in acceptance at Rome, but Linus may well have been the most prominent among the presbyters of Rome, at a time after this fragment (though not as a fragment) was written.

2 Timothy ends with a greeting to Timothy: 'The Lord be with thy spirit', and to the church: 'Grace be with you' (in the plural).

1. *Should christians love this present world-age? Is there a limit?*

2. *Has the inspiring Spirit, 2 Tim 3:16, a care for cloaks, books and parchments?*

3. *Do the papal claims stand and fall by the succession of a line of monarchical bishops at Rome from Peter onwards?*

7

The letter to Titus
Tit 1:1–3:15

Tit 1:1–4. The opening address

Paul calls himself 'servant of Jesus Christ', Rom 1:1;
cf Phil 1:1, rather than 'servant of God', cf James 1:1.
It is, of course, an OT conception, especially used of
prophets, Am 3:7. The parallel with 'apostle of Jesus
Christ'—Paul normally has 'apostle of Christ Jesus',
1 Cor 1:1 etc—makes the prophetic parallel particularly
relevant. The purpose of apostolic work is faith, cf Rom
1:5, in hope of eternal life, cf Rom 6:22–23. Faith is
equated here with 'knowledge of the truth which accords
with godliness', the traditional pattern of christian truth
in which all converts are instructed, cf 1 Tim 2:4;
1 Tim 3:15 (and right through the pastorals). There is a
parallel statement about God's gift to us in Christ before
the ages and the fulfilment at the appropriate, and
recently past, time in 2 Tim 1:9–10; here the theme is
worked out in terms of promise and manifestation. God's
word which is manifested in the preaching is the gospel
concerning his Son, promised beforehand through his
prophets, Rom 1:1–3. Paul has been entrusted with this
preaching, 1 Tim 2:7; 2 Tim 1:11. God is saviour,
cf 1 Tim 1:1; 2:3, a favourite word in the pastorals,
probably with an eye to the cult of the emperor as saviour.
   Titus is well known from the certain Paulines, Gal

2:1–3; 2 Cor 2:12–13; 7:5–16; 8:6, 16–23; 12:18. 'My true child' indicates that Titus was Paul's convert: that is fully compatible with the picture given of him in Gal 2 as an uncircumcised christian of pagan Greek origin. The 'common' faith is presumably that of ex-pagan christians like Titus and Jewish christians like Paul.

In the greeting Christ Jesus is given the title of 'saviour', cf 2:13; 3:6. The transfer of the title is fully intelligible in the perspective of the pastorals, since Christ is the mediator between God the saviour and saved mankind, 1 Tim 2:3–5.

1. What continuity is there between the preaching entrusted to St Paul and that of the church today? How is continuity to be secured?

2. Is knowledge of the truth something that has to grow in personal christian living in terms of its intrinsic nature?

Tit 1:5–16. Titus' work in Crete

We were told at 1 Tim 1:3ff that Timothy had been urged to remain at Ephesus to care for the church there, and particularly in the matter of teaching, but also right across the range of church order, including the question of the appointment of church officers. Now we are told that Titus has been left in Crete to see to good order in all things, and in the first place in the appointment of church officers, but covering teaching and the whole of christian living also. If Nicopolis in 3:12 is the one in Epirus, the suggestion is that Paul has gone on there; but then the body of the letter supposes that Titus is going to remain in Crete, while the closing section, very likely a genuine fragment from Paul, summons him to Nicopolis.

Presbyters are to be appointed in every town—a phrase that unconsciously reflects the early christian missionary strategy of concentrating on the towns and leaving the countryside to countrymen; 'pagans' means just that. Much has been made of the plural 'presbyters', 1:5, and the singular 'bishop', 1:7. But in fact the shift from plural to singular occurs at the beginning of 1:6, certainly refers to presbyters, and is entirely natural. There is nothing to show that a presbyter is not equally a bishop, certainly nothing to show that each town has one bishop but several presbyters. Nor is it clear what the 'for' is doing in 1:7 if we are not being given a single consistent list of qualities. 'Blameless' is the equivalent of 'above reproach' of 1 Tim 3:2, and the whole lists are very closely parallel, where they are not identical. Where 1 Tim 3:5 established a parallel between stewardship of a man's own household and of God's church, Tit 1:7 defines the essential role of the presbyter-bishop as that of stewardship under God; in 1 Cor 4:1–2 Paul had defined apostleship in similar fashion. Where 1 Tim 3:2 is content with laying it down that the bishop must be an apt teacher, Tit 1:9 expands this in terms of faithfulness to traditional teaching, knowledge of sound doctrine and ability to refute objections. It is most unlikely that that is a requirement for the construction of fundamental theological arguments in the style of Paul; an example of what the author has in mind is given in 1:10–16.

The quotation cited against Cretans in 1:12, identified in antiquity as from Epimenides of Knossos, of the sixth century BC, ties down this particular group of false teachers. But for the rest, their teaching, described only in general terms, seems the same sort of stuff we met with in 1 Timothy. There is the same Jewish background, cf 1:10 with 1 Tim 1:7; the same reference to myths,

cf 1 Tim 1:4; 4:7, and a similar empty wordiness, 1:10
and 1 Tim 6:4. Once again they are accused of being
greedy for money, 1:11, cf 1 Tim 6:5–10; they are cor-
rupt in mind and conscience, cf 1 Tim 4:2; 6:5, and are
totally confused about pure and impure, cf 1 Tim 4:3.
They claim to have a special knowledge of God, cf 1 Tim
6:20, but deny him in their manner of life, cf 2 Tim 3:
4–5.

It looks very much as if 'Paul' has in fact no direct
knowledge of the doctrinal situation in Crete. The kind
of false teaching reflected in the pastorals, a kind of pre-
gnosticism with a Jewish background and connections,
was likely to emerge wherever there were christian communities with Jewish connections or interests. Against all
such unorthodoxies the pastorals affirm the sound faith,
the approved truth of orthodox christian tradition, 1:
13–14.

*1. What kind of theological knowledge should be re-
quired, do you think, of a priest in a parish?*
2. Who are the empty talkers of today, if any?

Tit 2:1–10. Advice for different groups

This section, like 1 Tim 5:1–6:2, Col 3:18–4:1, and
other passages in the letters, is a piece of ethical advice
addressed to different groups within the community, men
and women, young and old, slave and free; in this instance
the advice is mediated through the church official responsible for sound doctrine. Such pieces of necessarily bland
and general moral advice were much in vogue in Greek
pagan moral writing. In these circumstances, such passages are inevitably flat and dull, unless the transforming
leaven of christianity can be seen to be at work upon

them. To be temperate, serious and sensible, chaste, domestic and kind, to show integrity, gravity and sound speech, are surely moral necessities in any sound community; but these are not qualities to set the world aflame. Nor are obedience, singleness of heart, justice and fairness, not simply in terms of the words used; but Paul knew how to save the basic from degenerating into the anodyne: 'Masters, treat your slaves justly and fairly, knowing that you have a master in heaven', Col 3:22–4:1. In comparison, the specifically christian touches in this passage of Titus tend to suffer from their moralising surroundings. Faith, love and steadfastness (a practical equivalent to hope) are in danger of becoming three moral qualities among others, rather than a three-fold statement of the basic character of christian existence. The word of God that could be discredited is not the same all-powerful word of Heb 4:12. The submissiveness and satisfactoriness of the slaves adorn a doctrine of God our saviour that is curiously lacking in saltiness towards slave-owners.

1. Can the responsibility of the christian teacher be fulfilled in the moral sphere through a set of ethical generalisations ('bourgeois' if you like) of this kind?

2. What should be the primary areas of christian moral concern in our own society?

Tit 2:11–3:8. The basis of christian hope

This passage is closely linked to the rather disappointing section preceding it: christian ethics depends totally upon God's grace, and grace anticipates glory. The language is liturgical in tone, and at 3:4–7 there is, in all probability, a direct quotation from a baptismal liturgy. The theology of the pastorals is richer and fuller the closer it comes to liturgical sources.

God's grace is incarnate grace, that undergoes epiphany ('appeared') in the humanity of Jesus. Its scope is universal with the universality of God's saving will, cf 1 Tim 2:4. Grace involves growth, the training in righteousness that is the task of scripture, 2 Tim 3:16, and a renunciation of worldly passions, those that limit and restrain us from the ever-expanding future of God. Sobriety, uprightness and godliness take on fresh life and a new dimension in this eschatological context where everything points forward to the epiphany of Christ in glory. The glory is that of our great God-and-saviour Jesus Christ—this is almost certainly one of the rare NT passages where the word 'God' is transferred to Jesus. The eschatological context helps to make this appropriate; it is at the last end of the world that God will be all in all, 1 Cor 15:28. Jesus is saviour as the one who gave himself for us even unto death, Gal 2:20, that he might redeem us from all iniquity as a new Israel, cf Ps 130:8, to purify for himself a people of his own, as God took Israel at Sinai, cf Ex 19:5; Deut 14:2. Election is the source and cause of a christian pattern of life.

The minister of the church must faithfully teach christian ethics and their basis, with a full authority; no one is to take his position lightly. The emphatic statement, and the echo of 1 Tim 4:12, suggest that the authority of the ministry was not going unquestioned at this stage in its development, a generation and more after Paul's time. Church writers, most of them themselves ordained men, have usually supposed that an unquestioned acceptance of ministerial authority would solve all problems; and to find all too ready a connection between submission to church authorities and secular powers. There is just such

a connection between 2:15 and 3:1. The duty of obedience to state authority is urged in Rom 13:1–7, cf 1 Pet
2:13–17; but Jesus' sayings in the gospels seem to hold a
mordant irony, Mk 12:13–17, and Revelation is written
out of a church which experienced the empire as a satanic
power, 17:1–18. Here the exhortation to civic obedience
leads into a general call to good deeds and peaceableness.

One established theme of christian moral preaching is
the contrast between 'then' and 'now', cf 1 Cor 6:9–11;
what had earlier been a piece of direct personal experience, however touched up and dramatised, has now
turned into a moral account of the changeover from the
old pagan world to the new world ushered in through the
life and death of Jesus. The incarnation is the epiphany
in a human life of the goodness and 'philanthropy'—
words applied to the Roman emperors in contemporary
inscriptions—of God our saviour. The contrast between
human deeds done in righteousness and God's mercy is
clearly based upon St Paul's basic and sharp distinction
between God's gift and man's deserving, faith in Christ
and the works of the law. It has sometimes been thought
that the expression of the distinction here is clumsy and
un-Pauline, but in Phil 3:6–9 Paul first lays claim to a
righteousness under the law before going on to reject self-
righteousness in favour of righteousness from God. God's
mercy is communicated to us by baptism, the bath
(cf Eph 5:26) of rebirth-and-renewal-in-the-Spirit. Baptism is rebirth, as also birth from above, in Jn 3:3, 7. The
word used here, *palingenesia*, was used by stoic writers for
the periodic renewal of the world after each world-age
had ended in destruction by fire; Philo the Jew had
applied it to the recreation of the world after the flood of
Genesis. It is used in description of the 'new world' in
Mt 19:28, the new world at the last end of time. 1 Pet 1:3,

a passage identified by Boismard as part of a baptismal hymn, also speaks of being born anew through the resurrection of Christ. The immediate background to Tit 3:5 therefore is Jewish and christian; there is no need to look to the Greek mystery-religions, as scholars have suggested.

Baptism means the gift of the Spirit, poured out— perhaps a reminiscence of anointing, Lk 4:18, cf Rom 5:5, Joel 2:28—with a view to making those baptised heirs of God, Gal 4:5–7, destined for eternal life, sealed for it already with hope, cf 2 Cor 1:22, justified already by grace, Rom 3:24.

This 'sure saying', not so much proverbial as liturgical, links together in this way so many baptismal themes from Paul and the NT catechesis. Notice, too, the underlying Trinitarian pattern of 3:4–6, and compare it with the Trinitarian baptismal formula of Mt 28:19.

1. Is it a desirable thing that authority within the church should go unchallenged? Has it ever done so?

2. How does one distinguish between true and false reform in the church? Is even true reform likely without authority feeling challenged?

3. Is an alliance between throne and altar, or their equivalents, a necessity of christian society?

Tit 3:8b–11. Controversy and discipline

The letter moves towards its end with a further reminder about the need for moral teaching, given in very general terms. There follows a warning about what to avoid, obviously a last warning about false teaching which has so often been described as wordy controversy, 1 Tim 6:4, a question of genealogies, 1 Tim 1:4, quarrels over the law, 1 Tim 1:7. The rule given for dealing with a factious man, a party man (the word is the fore-runner of the later

'heretic') is similar to that given in Mt 18:15–17. The
ultimate justification for excommunication is that the
obstinate party man has already condemned himself by
separating himself from the doctrine of the church community.

Where does personal theory become sectarian opinion?
Must we always be ready to drop a theory when this is
demanded by church authority?

Titus 3:12–15. A fragment from Paul

Tychicus is familiar to us from 2 Tim 4:12; Col 4:7–8;
Eph 6:21. Artemas is otherwise unknown, a mark pointing to the authenticity of this passage. Paul is obviously
engaged in missionary journeyings, and has decided to
winter at Nicopolis, a fairly frequent name for a town,
but it is likely that the one in Epirus is meant. Titus, if
indeed this fragment was part of a letter to him, is recalled
to Paul's side.

Zenas the lawyer is another unknown; perhaps he had
acted as Paul's postman, along with Apollos. Apollos is
presumably the well-known and brilliant Alexandrian of
1 Cor 1:12 etc, and introduced with a description of his
abilities in Ac 18:24–28. Since Luther's time it has often
been thought that he was the author of Hebrews, a work
with Alexandrian affinities.

The fragment ends with a word of general moral
exhortation, the first part anticipated at 3:8 above, and
with final greetings. In 'Grace be with you all', 'you' is
plural, showing that the letter was addressed through
Titus to a whole church community.

Is it true that the 'cases of urgent need' will always be
with us? What do we do about them?

Revelation

John Challenor

Introduction

From AD 81 till 96 Domitian ruled the Roman empire in which all christians lived. Domitian was not the first emperor to persecute christians. Nero (54–68) had been first, putting the blame for a fire in Rome on the church in that city. But Domitian was the first emperor to call himself *Dominus et Deus*—'Lord and God'—and to demand from his subjects all over the empire, by edict, that they recognise and worship him by the burning of incense and the pouring of a libation in front of his statue.

With this requirement, as contrary to the first commandment and as giving to Caesar what belongs to God, christians were unable to comply. In Asia Minor (present-day Turkey) there seems to have been popular pressure put on christians to conform, and the local imperial officials moved more energetically than elsewhere to enforce the directives on emperor-worship. Christian non-participation was conspicuous. Persecution in the law-courts followed, with charges of treason, atheism, and membership of an illegal organisation. (Jews too were unable to obey this law, but over the centuries they had won exemption from imperial laws repugnant to their faith. Earlier when christianity had appeared to the world to be a variant of judaism, christians had shared the exemption. But when christianity became distinct from judaism, christians were not influential enough—or not innocuous enough—to keep the exemption which the Jews continued to enjoy.)

In Revelation an acute conflict of the churches with the state and civil society is reflected. In Acts and the NT letters, christians appear as having a quarrel with the Jews but as law-abiding loyalists towards Rome and society generally. In Revelation, there are reflections of a real detestation of Rome and the Roman social order. In Revelation we see churches marked by a (non-violent) revolutionary attitude towards the whole existing structure of political and social life.

About the year 95, it seems, a christian pastor we know as John was exiled by the government to the off-shore island of Patmos in the Aegean Sea. There he wrote the book called Revelation. Probably he had been working in Ephesus, the capital of the Roman proconsular province of Asia, and wrote the book for the church in Ephesus, and for six other neighbouring churches, and ultimately for all the church.

He calls the book his *apocalypsis*, a Greek word meaning something brought out of hiding, a disclosure, a revelation, an apocalypse. Writings in this category of apocalyptic are fairly common in Jewish and christian circles between about 200 BC and 100 AD. Some of them are in the bible—for example, Daniel 7–12, Isaiah 24–27, parts of Zechariah and Joel, and Mark 13 and its parallels. Others are outside the canon—for example, the books of Enoch, 2 Esdras and the Apocalypse of Peter.

Apocalyptic writing is particularly concerned with the future of the world, the end of history, life after death, the last things—with, in a word, eschatology. Apocalyptic writers make plentiful use of imagery and symbolism and generally picture the inbreaking of God's final judgement and kingdom in and through violent cosmic cataclysms.

Apocalypses were written and avidly read especially in times of crisis and persecution. Apocalyptic is in fact prophecy highly developed in one direction. Both prophecy and apocalyptic convey the word and will of God. When prophecy died out in Israel after the return from the exile, it was apocalyptic that took its place. That Jesus himself made use of apocalyptic language is clear from Mk 14:62 and from Mk 13 and its parallels. St Paul expresses apocalyptic expectations of the end in 1 Thes 4.

As the footnotes of any full edition show, Revelation draws very extensively on OT prophecy and apocalyptic. A count has revealed that no fewer than 278 out of the 404 verses of the book contain some excerpt from the canonical OT. (The quotation is always free, never verbatim.) And this is apart from John's considerable use of apocryphal sources. This heavy dependence of Revelation on OT tradition (as well as on the transforming fulfilment of it brought about by Christ) means that the book is best studied, as it stands in the canon, last. Again and again, the puzzling phrase or image in Revelation is a standard OT phrase or image, or an allusion to some parallel OT situation, which provides the key to John's meaning. The OT is the dictionary which enables us to decipher John's message, translating his pictorial images feature by feature into the corresponding mental ideas.

It is not certain that Revelation was written as a single work all at once. Some scholars think Revelation as we have it is two apocalypses of different dates edited together as one, and they have tried to clarify some of the obscurities in the text by separating the two out again. Others have tried to see more light by rearranging the order of the material in other ways. But no convincing case has yet been made for a change, and this commentary takes the text as we have it.

Who was John of Patmos? Some early MSS of the NT
ascribe Revelation to 'John the theologian' or 'John the
divine'. Some early church writers identify him with
John the son of Zebedee, one of the twelve, and with the
author of the fourth gospel and three NT letters of John.
Many say today that in language especially, and to a lesser
extent in theology, Revelation differs so strikingly from
the gospel and letters of John that it simply could not be
by the same author. John of Patmos presents himself as a
prophet, not an apostle, and when he speaks of the twelve
in Rev 21:14 he speaks of them as if they were quite
remote from himself.

Who John of Patmos was, we shall probably never
know. Probably more useful than sifting the inconclusive
evidence yet again is to remember that the 'Johannine'
books of the NT—gospel, letters, apocalypse—all seem to
emerge from the tradition as developed in and around
Ephesus, where Paul spent two or three years about 55
and founded a church (Ac 19–20).

John's Revelation seems to have achieved immediate
and wide popularity. Professor Klaus Koch has given a
big surprise to christians today (who probably read and
use Revelation least of all the NT books) by showing that
in the christian writings of the second century that have
survived, Revelation is the NT book most frequently
quoted. Later, when the church expressed the faith rather
in terms of Greek philosophy than Jewish apocalyptic,
and made peace with the Roman empire, christians found
Revelation foreign and uncongenial. When the limits of
the NT canon were agreed, late in the fourth century,
Revelation was admitted only with some difficulty; in
parts of the east, it was not accepted for another two
centuries.

The main point to bear in mind while reading Revelation is that John wrote it for a pastoral purpose—to give courage and hope to persecuted christians by reassuring them that Christ's victory over the evil of the world was in no doubt, and that God was certainly going to vindicate his people by showing his hand publicly to the world.

Book list

In addition to the Jerome Commentary (which gives a full bibliography) and the Jerusalem Bible notes, there is G. B. Caird's *Commentary on Revelation* (1966) in A. & C. Black's NT series, a full-length book and very useful. Austin Farrer: *A Rebirth of Images* (1949) has a high reputation, like its author. Hubert Richards: *What the Spirit Says to the Churches* (1967) is a very helpful short outline. Klaus Koch: *The Rediscovery of Apocalyptic* (1972) is a short study of the present evaluation of apocalyptic, and Mathias Rissi: *The Future of the World* (1972) is a short but detailed study of the last four chapters of Revelation.

On the political side, see Oscar Cullmann: *The State in the New Testament* (1957), and W. H. C. Frend: *Martyrdom and Persecution in the Early Church* (1965). Norman Cohn: *The Pursuit of the Millennium* (1957) studies the influence of Revelation in church and social history.

On the problem of time, in relation to the finality of Christ's saving acts—a problem raised acutely in Revelation—Oscar Cullmann: *Christ and Time* (3rd edition 1962) is always helpful.

1

Letters to the Asian churches
Rev 1:1–3:22

Rev 1:1–3. 'What must soon take place' (a phrase borrowed from Dan 2:28) is in effect the sub-title of Revelation and a description of the contents of the book. This sub-title is expanded in 1:19 to 'what you see, what is and what is to take place hereafter'.

What is to take place? The book will go on to describe a series of visions of heaven, and a series of calamities, partly historical and partly cosmic, including particularly a wave of persecution of the church, leading to the second coming of Christ, the final victory of God, and the renewal of creation.

Did John mean his readers to take him quite literally? If he did, it seems he expected soon the total dissolution of the world-order he knew, and its unmistakable replacement by a new kingdom, that of God. Or did John mean to be taken in some measure metaphorically? If he did, did he make use of the traditional apocalyptic imagery of the violent death-throes of the old world preceding the inbreaking of the new, in such a way as to explain and interpret the violent conflict impending as he wrote—persecution and martyrdom on the mainland—as a sign of the coming of Christ?

It is not at all easy to say whether John was writing literally, or metaphorically and mythologically, or even if he was conscious of a clear choice. The time to try to answer the question is after reading the book. Meanwhile it is worth noting that only two or three generations after John wrote, Montanus and an ascetic group of followers known as the Montanists took John literally on at least one important point. They went from the area of the seven churches up-river to Pepuza in Phrygia and waited, convinced that the new Jerusalem spoken of by John at Rev 21:2 would soon descend there from the sky. (By AD 200 Montanism was condemned as a heretical movement.)

'He who reads aloud', and 'those who hear' are the christian community assembled for the liturgy. John's book is not for any restricted circle of specialists: it is for all christians. The 'time' (*kairos*) is the time of Christ's coming.

Rev 1:4–8. The greeting is similar to those in NT letters. The seven churches are not all the churches in Asia Minor: we know from the NT and from Ignatius of Antioch that there were more. John may have chosen seven as the number symbolising totality, or he may have chosen the seven he knew best, or he may have chosen the seven located in towns which had a law-court where christians could be tried.

By the seven spirits John could mean the seven archangels of judaism, but more likely (between the Father and Christ) he means the Holy Spirit, sevenfold in his perfection and gifts (Is 11:2). The first description of Jesus as 'witness' (or martyr; the same Greek word *martys* covers both) indicates John's preoccupation with martyrdom.

Rev 1:9–20. This section is comparable to the accounts of the calling and commissioning of OT prophets. The close association in 1:9—the simultaneity and even virtual identity—of suffering and glory, suggests the theology of the fourth gospel, in which Christ's crucifixion is also his glorification.

'In the Spirit' seems to mean in a trance or ecstasy. Ezekiel spoke of being taken by the Spirit when he experienced a power beyond his own, using him and guiding him (Ez 2:14). It is another question whether John means he really was transported outside the order of ordinary faith and prayer and worship, or whether he is utilising the literary device of the supernatural vision which was conventional in apocalyptic writing. 'On the Lord's day' means at the Sunday liturgy.

The seven golden lampstands are the seven churches. Present in them is the risen Christ pictured in a variety of OT terms which identify him as messiah and associate him with the Father. (The sharp two-edged sword is a symbol from Is 11:4 and 49:2.) The seven stars, or the angels of the churches (1:20) may be guardian angels thought of as responsible for, and reprehensible for, local affairs. Or they may be the presbyters or bishops who oversee the churches, but this is less likely, since there is no known use of 'angel' in this sense. John is using metaphors, in any case: for all practical purposes, the seven stars, the seven lampstands, and the seven angels all stand for the seven churches.

The important thing is the assurance with which the chapter ends—that the churches are in the hand of Christ. This is to strengthen and cheer up those who see persecution and suffering impending.

What is there, in the language which John chooses to speak of God and Christ, which is calculated to help his fellow christians on the mainland?

Rev 2:1–7. The letters to the seven churches occupy chapters 2 and 3. Each of the seven letters is cast in the same form—a description of Christ, author of the words of the letter, an assessment of the church's work and witness, and in most cases some promise of reward. A sort of visitation or review seems to be taking place, to see how far each church is fit and ready to stand up to the coming ordeal. Nearly all the letters contain detailed allusions to particular local circumstances.

Ephesus wins praise for having rejected teachers who falsely claimed some apostolic authority. (They would hardly have claimed to have been members of the twelve.) Possibly, in the struggle for correct doctrine, the church had lost some of the fraternal love experienced by Paul from church leaders from Ephesus (Ac 20:36–38).

About the Nicolaitans little is known for certain. It seems that they favoured participation in the religious feasts of pagans, eating meat sacrificed to idols, contrary to the agreement of Ac 15:29. They seem to have exaggerated christian freedom to a point where it became a sort of moral lawlessness. 'He who conquers' is everyone who endures to martyrdom.

Rev 2:8–11. For the church at Smyrna, Christ has only praise. It was materially poor—perhaps as a result of separating itself from pagan society—but rich in faith. Some hostility came from Jews, who were not of the true Israel since they rejected the messiah. The church was to expect a persecution—a short test, with a happy outcome, if the allusion is to the ten days of Dan 1:12. The faithful and steadfast will survive the danger of the second death —damnation after natural death.

Rev 2:12–17. Pergamum had a temple of the emperor-cult—'Satan's throne'. 'Antipas my witness' (martyr) is

the firmest evidence in Revelation that persecution to
death had actually begun.

The complaint is that the Pergamum church includes
members who cooperate in pagan religion following the
teaching of Balaam and the teaching of the Nicolaitans.
These are not two teachings, but one: the sense of 2 : 15
is 'in this way you too, like the Ephesians, have some who
hold the teaching of the Nicolaitans'. Balaam had encouraged Israel in the desert to join in the false worship
of the Moabites and fornicate with Moabite women. The
immorality of 2 : 14 is basically idolatry, or unfaithfulness
to the covenant relationship with God, but it may well
include sexual promiscuity.

The first great practical issue to come to a head in the
christian churches as a whole had been about their relation to Israel, and how gentile and Jewish christians could
co-exist. The second great issue was over the attitude
christians should adopt towards governments, and how
far they should cooperate with the non-christian establish-
ment in society. Paul years earlier had argued that eating
meat sacrificed to idols could be a stumbling block for
one's fellow-christians. But he had also realised that a
complete break with the pagan milieu would mean in
theory leaving the world altogether (1 Cor 5 : 10). In
practice, the attempt tends to make the church into an
exclusive sect.

And what about the churches and the secular government? Had not Paul urged obedience to the governing
authorities as instituted by God (Rom 13 : 1)? Did not the
Lukan writings present the agents and officers of the
Roman state in a good light? Did not Jesus himself speak
of giving Caesar his due?

The Nicolaitans then may plausibly have asked, why is
our brother John in these letters being more rigorous

than the tradition as we know it? John's answer must have been, in a word, persecution. The state was now hostile, taken over by demonic powers. Leaving aside the short opportunist persecution of Nero, which was confined to Rome, christians now faced a new situation, and the refrain 'let him hear what the Spirit says to the churches' probably refers to this new sign of the times.

An event of modern history is relevant. In 1933 the German chancellor, Hitler, decreed the exclusion from the German churches of all who were of Jewish descent, and required the churches to colour their preaching with nazi ideology in the form of patriotic nationalism. An appreciable minority of the evangelical church was convinced that to comply would be to fall into heresy. Their leaders met in May 1934 at Barmen, and drafted the Barmen declaration which drew a clear line between the gospel and the powers and ideas of this world. A 'confessing' church came into existence, deliberately separating itself from the main body which it judged to have betrayed the gospel. The Barmen declaration became the main charter of christian resistance to nazism. At the service with which the Barmen meeting opened, the preacher spoke on the text of Rev 2:1–7.

To return to the church at Pergamum: that church must turn from its undue tolerance, its indifferentism. The persevering faithful will earn everlasting life, pictured as a share in the heavenly manna and as an admission ticket to the messianic supper.

Rev 2:18–29. Thyatira was noted for its trade associations and guilds. (Ac 16 mentions a saleswoman from there, in Europe.) Probably christians in Thyatira faced a hard choice: either share in the pagan observances of local religious life, or accept a painful degree of social

ostracism and poverty. In this situation, the gifted Jezebel
had a following, for teaching similar to that of the Nicolaitans. The adultery is probably metaphorical—a following of false teaching.

   *1. How do we judge where to draw the line between
the church and the world?*
   *2. Is it possible for christians to overstress orthodoxy at
the expense of love? And vice versa?*

Rev 3:1–6. The church at Sardis has perhaps already
made its compromise with 'the world'. Whatever the explanation, it is almost dead, but not quite—a minority
satisfy John's standards.
   'He who conquers' or 'he who is victorious' is a recurring phrase. It always means primarily the martyr who
sheds his or her blood for Christ.

Rev 3:7–13. The open door may be special missionary
opportunities (perhaps among Jews), or it may be the
ordinary christian call to new life, or it may be both. The
small church at Philadelphia seems to have met hostility
from Jews who, rejecting the messiah, are not the true
Israel and are indeed a synagogue of Satan. There is
another formula in 3:10—'those who dwell upon the
earth'—which keeps recurring in Revelation. From the
contexts it becomes clear that John means the world in so
far as it is hostile to God and Christ. (The fourth gospel
uses the term *kosmos*, world, in this way.) 'Those who
dwell upon the earth' are those who are not the people of
God. The people of the world tend to be subject, like the
Egyptians in Exodus, to plagues from which God's people
are exempted.

Rev 3:14–22. The church at Laodicea too seems to have
succumbed to worldliness. (Lukewarm drinks tend to be

*Our Lady of
Consolation,
Pray for Us*

Marian Year
June 1987-August 1988

The Consolata
Missionaries sincerely
thank you for sharing
in their missionary
endeavors.

They gratefully
pray to Our Lady of
Consolation for You,
your Family, and all
your loved ones.

Consolata Missionaries
P.O. Box 5550
Somerset, N.J. 08875
(201) 297-9191

nauseating.) Scathing as this report is, there is no question of rejection or breaking off of relations. Instead, there is a warm invitation to repent, and to re-admit Christ into the life of the church.

The coming of Christ in 3:20 is pictured in terms which embrace (1) the presence of Christ with the believer (Jn 14:23); (2) the eucharist (Mk 14:25); (3) the messianic banquet of the end (Mt 8:11); (4) the parousia (Mt 24:33). And all these are closely interconnected (1 Cor 11:26).

1. How would the local church you belong to react to serious criticism of the sort found in Rev 2 and 3?

2. Can you think of anyone in the church today corresponding to John of Patmos, as he has revealed himself so far?

3. What is the Spirit saying to the churches today? How do we know?

4. How is Christ present in his church?

2

Events before the end
Rev 4:1–16:21

Rev 4:1–11. The address from which John writes is still Patmos, and the date is still the Lord's day (1:10). After the survey of the life of the churches on earth, the angel (or is it Christ himself?—see 1:10–12) now takes John up to heaven to show him from there how God is in supreme control of the calamitous events preceding his final victory.

Dr Caird, in his recent commentary, has a helpful analogy. He says, imagine the war control-room at supreme headquarters. An officer moves symbols on maps. Sometimes he is recording changes reported inwards from the fronts; at other times he records movements and operations ordered outwards to the fronts. The former is descriptive symbolism, and the latter is determinative symbolism. John's symbols in Revelation are like the officer's symbols: they are the pictorial heavenly counterparts of earthly happenings. And if you think the military nature of the parallel unsuitable, recall that John is thinking in terms of a cosmic confrontation between the powers of good and evil, light and darkness.

Heaven is the place of God's power. John visualises it in terms of a royal throne-room, of the Jerusalem temple (the associations in 4:8), of a synagogue (the scroll, 5:1), and perhaps also of a court of law. John makes no use here of terms belonging to the christian eucharistic celebration, but since 1:10 remains operative he may be indicating in a more comprehensive way that the eucharist is the way in to an understanding of the mysteries of God.

The throne is the chief symbol of God's power—a reassuring symbol for christians in a world otherwise dominated by Caesar's throne, or Satan's. By likening the divine presence to precious stones, John associates God with light, colour, and magnificence. Allusion to the noises that accompanied God's appearance at Sinai evokes his power. The seven spirits again probably signify the sevenfold Holy Spirit.

The twenty-four elders (presbyters—the word from which 'priest' derives) probably symbolise the people of God as a whole—the twelve tribes of the old Israel and the twelve of the new.

The sea of glass seems at first to be part of the splendid ornamentation, but in mainstream Hebrew tradition the sea is a symbol of evil, and here it may stand between God and man until the end, when 'the sea was no more'. (Rev 21:1.)

The four living creatures, Babylonian in origin, are spoken of by Ezekiel as figures supporting God's throne, and here John merges them with Isaiah's seraphim to lead the worship of God.

Their song (4:11) asserts what the first commandment requires, and implies that no earthly emperor may be worshipped.

This chapter, which sets the scene, should be read together with the next, which describes the action.

Rev 5:1–7. The scroll and the writing that completely covers it represents God's saving plan for his creation. The scroll has seven seals, so it is perfectly closed, absolutely secret. There is a pause full of suspense. Who is able to understand and willing to implement God's plan? John weeps with anxiety, knowing the physical and mental sufferings of persecuted christians. Left to himself, without intelligible explanation, man's life in the world can be a torment of meaninglessness. If no one can be found to shoulder the responsibility, will God's plan remain indefinitely sealed up and without effect? But someone worthy is found; an elder points to Christ, who has 'conquered'.

This 'conquered', in the once-for-all past tense, is of prime importance for understanding Revelation. It refers to Christ's victory on the cross, the victorious death which has already undermined and defeated evil. Whatever lurid battle-scenes unfold in later chapters of Revelation, there is no further decisive battle in the future of which the outcome might be in doubt; there are only mopping-up operations. Whatever pictures of vindictive retribution Revelation may seem to paint, there is none, for Christ's victory is the Calvary victory and the rising again.

Christ appears as a lamb slaughtered, but with full power and knowledge (the horns and eyes). The lion of Judah is the lamb of God, victorious through serving and suffering.

Rev 5:8–14. One important feature of this hymn of praise to Christ is the reign of God's people already on earth (5:10). It is not Caesar and his military men and his bureaucracy who rule; against all appearances it is the harassed fugitive church, in which the power of God in Christ is at work.

1. What is it that makes the eucharistic celebration the privileged way of understanding the mysteries of God's will?

2. *Did John take too serious a view of emperor-worship? Could he not have treated it as a formality, rather as christians in Britain now subscribe happily to the legal fiction of constitutional law that the king (or queen) can do no wrong? (Chapters 4 and 5 may suggest part of John's answer.)*

Rev 6:1–8. The opening of the scroll unleashes a series of disasters like those predicted in the gospel apocalypse as coming before the end (Mk 13 and parallels). John is saying that all that happens on earth is according to God's plan, and that human sin still involves opposition to the kingdom (as it involved opposition to Jesus in his earthly ministry), and hence adverse judgement.

The four horses, white, red, black and putrid in colour, are borrowed from Zechariah 6. But it is the four riders who are important here, and they are John's own symbol. They represent invasion, war, famine, and plague—more or less as these are mentioned in Lk 21:10–11.

John's four horsemen all seem to have some basis in historical events. In the late first century the Parthians invaded the Empire in the east. A series of wars ensued. There was a corn shortage in 92, according to the historian Suetonius. Grain was at famine prices, a day's bread ration costing a day's earnings. Oil and wine and various luxuries remained plentiful. Suetonius tells us there was popular resistance to government pressure to plough up vineyards and sow more corn. And plague was inseparable from undernourishment and the movement of armies. John's purpose is to embrace within the same series events already experienced and events yet to come, to help him assure the reader that the events to come really will happen.

Rev 6:9–11. The martyrs John sees are presumably recent Asian martyrs and Roman martyrs of Nero's reign

a generation earlier. For this scene John visualises the
altar of the Jerusalem temple under which the blood of
sacrificed animals used to flow. The martyrs' question
'how long?' is exactly the question John is answering in
Revelation.

Taken as they stand in translation, the words 'avenge
our blood' may present a problem about sentiments of
revenge in christians who are supposed to forgive and
love their enemies. In the Greek the word is the one used
in Jesus's parable of the unjust judge (Lk 18:1–8), where
it is translated 'vindicate' or 'do justice'. Possibly John
uses the word here as part of the language of Israel's
everyday law. Alternatively, he may really mean revenge
(as RSV, JB, and NEB all take it) and if so you have to seek
some other solution—if you think there is a problem.

Meanwhile the martyrs receive a white robe (cf Rev 3:
4–5) and are told to wait patiently for the full imple-
mentation of God's plan.

The martyrs' question 'how long?' is the burning
question for John and his contemporaries. Is the faith
for which christians were about to be put to death well-
founded? Was the church correct in its evaluation of the
world situation in general and of the events of AD 95 in
particular? Those for whom martyrdom is an immediate
possibility are right, like St Thomas More, to sift the data
and weigh the issues as carefully as possible.

Rev 6:12–17. The cosmic earthquake which follows the
breaking of the sixth seal is a symbol of the coming of the
Lord in judgement of sinners. The references show that
John is drawing on the general stock of OT imagery (as the
evangelists do in the gospel apocalypse). By listing seven
features of nature, and seven classes of men, John is saying that the totality of creation is shaken.

Rev 7:1–3. From that dark picture of God's judgement on sinners, John turns abruptly to paint a joyful picture of the saving of the faithful. (Note that the seventh seal has yet to be broken.)

The number four indicates cosmic completeness; the four destructive winds correspond to some degree to the four horsemen. In the midst of the destruction unleashed by the breaking of the first six seals, a cosmic pause is ordered, so that God's servants may be marked— apparently to be saved from natural disaster in order to be available for martyrdom. The seal or mark put on them is not baptism. It is a mark borrowed from Ez 9, where in a parallel situation the Hebrew letter tau (T) was imposed on the righteous. (T, the last letter of the Hebrew alphabet, signified God, as did omega, the last letter of the Greek alphabet.) In the first century tau was written like a cross, hence the JB has 'mark a cross on their foreheads' at Ez 9:4. (Possibly John also has in mind Ex 12:23 where the blood of the passover lamb protects Israel from the destroying angel.)

Rev 7:4–8. The twelve tribes are not Israel, literally, but the whole church (cf Mt 19:28). The number of the saved is the complete number twelve multiplied by itself and expressed in thousands, signifying not the result of a census but an innumerable multitude. (John did not count them; he was told the number.)

Rev 7:9–17. Probably the 144,000 of 7:4 are identical with the great multitude of 7:9 (and 14:1), though possibly the 144,000 are christians on earth and the great multitude christians in heaven. Does John mean by the 144,000, or the multitude, or both, martyrs only, or saved christians in general? The language (7:14 especially) suggests he means martyrs. But from the letter to the church at Sardis, for example (3:4–5) it seems that John recognises other faithful christians as deserving to be clothed in white besides those who died as martyrs. For practical purposes it seems best to assume that John is speaking of the church as a whole—though it is a church led by the martyrs and headed by the faithful and true martyr-witness, Christ. We might say John is speaking of the whole by the part.

A reason for the uncertainty here may be that John is borrowing pictorial material from several sources, and does not trouble to make the resulting composite picture entirely consistent in itself. Much of the earlier part of Rev 7 comes from Ezekiel. Much of the later part comes from the apocalypse known as 2 Esdras, part of the OT apocrypha. 2 Esdras 2:38–45 reads as follows:

> See . . . the number of those who have been sealed . . .
> Zion, conclude the list of your people who have been
> clothed in white. I, Ezra, saw on Mount Zion a great
> multitude, praising the Lord with songs . . . Then I
> asked an angel, 'Who are these, my lord?' He answered,
> 'These are they who have put off mortal clothing, and
> have put on the immortal, and they have confessed the
> name of God; now they are being crowned, and receive
> palms'.

John draws in this chapter more heavily than ever on material of the OT period, apocalyptic and prophetic, canonical and apocryphal. He handles it to some degree as a familiar conventional literary form.

John makes two particular christian pastoral points. (1) In 7:15, God shelters the martyrs (the saved) with his presence. Literally, he 'will tent over them'. (2) In 7:17, the lamb whose wrath was equated with the wrath of God towards sinners (6:16) is now by contrast the shepherd of his servants.

Much of the material of John's visions is borrowed from earlier apocalyptic and prophetic writings. What are the implications of this fact?

Rev 8:1–5. As the seventh seal is opened, John expects his readers to be tense with expectancy for the climax to be revealed. But he defers the climax! He leads us through another sevenfold series, this time heralded by angels blowing trumpets. Apocalyptic does not proceed in logical, linear fashion from data to conclusion. Though events leading up to the end are chronological and can be listed in order, eschatological events are by definition outside the ordinary course of history and sequence of time, with the result that they can only be talked about with difficulty, with a strain upon our language. Revelation starts from the historical situation, but soon extrapolates. To deal with the mysterious end-events, John uses repetition, giving the same message first in one set of symbols, then in another, then again in a third.

Here, we go over the theme again in terms of the prayers of the saints and the punishment of their persecutors. The half-hour of silence in heaven is a pause in the otherwise incessant heavenly song of praise (4:8), to allow the prayers of the faithful on earth to get through and be heard. The prayers of all the saints—the church—are presented by an angel in a manner visualised in terms of Jewish temple worship.

Rev 8:6–12. The trumpets are associated in the OT with God's presence, and in the NT with the *parousia*. The first four trumpets herald plagues reminiscent of the ten plagues of the exodus story. The destruction of 'a third' is a conventional prophetic symbol indicating judgement and punishment for sin, but in such a way as to leave survivors who will, hopefully, repent. (Ez 5:12.) Only after the seventh trumpet will it be too late for repentance. The wormwood of 8:11 refers to Jer 9:15. These first four plagues affect nature—land, sea, fresh water, and sky—with disastrous results for human life.

Rev 8:13. Worse is to come. In the apocalypse of Baruch (77) an eagle speaks God's message. John seems to be borrowing this symbol to say that the next three calamities are going to be much worse than the first four.

Rev 9:1–11. The star (9:1) is an angel who opens the bottomless pit, the mythical underworld, the source of all evil. He unleashes a plague which is ostensibly of locusts but has also mixed within it the features of a plague of scorpions and of an invasion of Parthian cavalry. The imagery comes from Exodus and Joel, and from the apocryphal apocalypse of Enoch. Appalling as the picture is, the evil is still limited in extent and time (9:4–5). John sees it as limited to non-christians and to the five summer months of the locust's life.

Rev 9:12–21. The sixth plague breaks out in response to the prayers of Christ's disciples on earth. (This is clear from the mention of the altar in 9:13, read together with 8:3–4 and 6:9–10.) The historical basis of this plague is the Parthian cavalry from the east, the main military menace to the Roman Empire until the Emperor Trajan's victories over them in AD 114–116. But to this basis, John adds impressionistic features to indicate that by reason of sheer numbers and diabolical leadership this scourge is irresistible by any power except God's.

The Parthian mounted bowmen used to loose arrows at their enemy while galloping towards them, and then as they wheeled around and galloped away they would turn in the saddle and shoot again over their shoulders. This seems to be the point underlying 9:19.

In spite of these plagues, limited in extent to allow repentance, the survivors did not repent. The Lord waits. The discords remain to be resolved. The witness of the martyrs is still a pre-condition of God's final judgement and victory.

Rev 10:1–7. At this point, when the reader expects the seventh angel to blow the final trumpet, the climax is again postponed—till 11:15. Between the sixth and seventh trumpets (or the second and third woes for mankind) John inserts a vision of hope for christians, which is also a vision of hope for the world if it will repent.

'Another mighty angel' is the counterpart of the strong angel at 5:2. The first dealt with the large scroll, which contained God's plan for the world as the lamb was to put it into effect. This other angel brings a small scroll which contains the same plans in so far as the church on earth is to carry them out. The scroll is open: the message is the one John is giving to the churches—the interpretation he is putting on the signs of the times.

The seven thunders (10:4–5) are perhaps the voice of God with a message John is not to write down yet—the time for divulging this message comes later, at 22:10.

God is creator of the world (10:6). Implicitly, John here conveys that God loves all he has made. The mystery of God (10:7) is better translated God's secret intention or hidden purpose for creation. John shows here that God is not writing off the world as a whole. As in the fourth gospel, the world is twofold: there is the world God made and loves, and there is the world in so far as it opposes God's purpose for it. One of the church's chief theological and pastoral problems at every period is to try to know the mind of God, to discriminate, to judge how far to love the world and identify with it, and how far to hate the world and reject it. The church's witness can be dimmed both by too close a bond with the world and by too complete a rejection of it. Where the bond is too close the church becomes worldly, and implicated in evil. Where there is wholesale rejection the church easily becomes a negligible and eccentric sect. Our personal feelings, positive or negative, about the world around us influence our judgement and we ought to try to be aware of them.

Rev 10:8–11. John makes the message on the scroll his own and takes responsibility for it. The eating of the scroll is an image from Ez. 2:8. For John, as for Ezekiel, the word of God was sweet but the prophetic vocation of suffering entailed was bitter. Even at this late stage, John is commissioned to a prophetic ministry.

1. Explain the point of the eating of the little scroll.

2. Can a message of doom for the pagan world (ch 9) be a message of hope and encouragement for christians?

3. Examine the problem of forming and maintaining a christian relationship with the world. What individual personality factors have to be borne in mind?

Rev 11:1–13. Before the seventh trumpet sounds (11:15) there is another vision of the impending martyrdoms. The temple is the church, the living stones who are God's people. The innermost sanctuary of the church, which John measures, is safe, but all the rest which he does not measure is ravaged by persecution. The forty-two months, or 1,260 days, are the evil three years and a half of Daniel 7:25—'a time, two times, and half a time'. This was the period 168–165 BC when the pagan Greek ruler Antiochus Epiphanes tried to impose hellenistic culture on Israel. He occupied Jerusalem and desecrated the temple, putting an image of Zeus on the main altar.

JOHN PAUL'S VATICAN

Now On Video Cassette

Pope John Paul II has been to America, now you can visit the city where he lives without leaving your own home.

This card is your passport to "John Paul's Vatican," our unique look at life behind the walls of the Holy City. This 40-minute video cassette will introduce you to the people who live and work in the Mother Church. You'll meet:

★ The Altar Boys — They serve mass daily at St. Peter's
★ The Seminarians — American men studying in Rome
★ The Swiss Guards — They've been protecting Popes for centuries
★ The Curia — Clerics whose decisions affect 800 million lives
★ Plus many, many more

Feel the texture of life at the spiritual heart of Catholicism.
Visit places outsiders rarely glimpse.

★ Fascinating: The whole family will be awed and inspired
★ Educational: Learn about Catholicism and its history-rich capital

THE PERFECT CHRISTMAS GIFT FOR FAMILY AND FRIENDS

C.S.M.A.   ☐ English
10 Bay Street/Dept. 15   ☐ Spanish
Westport, CT 06880   ☐ VHS

Yes, please send me ___ VIDEOCASSETTE(S) of **John Paul's Vatican**
$29.95 each plus $3.00 shipping & handling.

Name _____
Address _____
City _____ State _____ Zip _____
☐ Check or money order enclosed.
☐ Bill my ☐ American Express ☐ Visa ☐ MasterCard
Card _____ Exp. Date _____
Signature _____

CC 1087

While persecution rages, the church testifies to Christ. The two witnesses, or olive-trees, or lampstands, stand for the people of God. The allusion is to Zech 4:14 where two leaders, Joshua and Zerubbabel, represent Israel. It is not yet the time of victory when they will appear in white garments, so they wear sackcloth. 11:5–6 refer to another two earlier witnesses—Moses and Elijah. John may have in mind also two later witnesses, Peter and Paul, martyred in Rome by Nero.

The beast embodies all the evil forces which oppose the witnessing church. For the evil period of three days and a half martyrs lie dead and exposed in the streets of Jerusalem and every worldly tyrannical city, particularly Rome. The worldly world rejoices at the death of the prophets. But God brings them to new life with an assumption into heaven like that of Elijah (2 Kg 2:11) and Moses (in the apocryphal *Assumption of Moses*). God brings disaster on the persecutors. The seven thousand who perish may be the counterpart of the seven thousand witnesses in the persecution Jezebel organised (1 Kg 19:18). Survivors repent and give glory to God: the work and witness of the martyrs bears fruit.

'The kingdom of heaven has suffered violence' (Mt 11:12). This section, and indeed Revelation as a whole, seems to be an extended commentary on those words of Jesus, and his corresponding words on the plundering and overcoming of the kingdom of Satan (Mt 12:28–29). Jesus seems to have meant that the kingdom of God is really at risk, and can suffer real defeat at any given time in any given place. Till the end, a real responsibility rests on Christ's disciples, always and everywhere.

Behind this long series of plagues and paroxysms and confrontations, which may by now be striking the reader as rather extravagant and superfluous, there is a genuine theological point. It is that evil must be eliminated from the world before the kingdom of God can come in its fullness.

Rev 11:14–18. There is no third woe, unless it is implicit, in judgement on sinners. The last trumpet heralds the setting up of the kingdom. This is the dénouement, or rather it is a brief preliminary glimpse of the dénouement. John arrives within sight of the end, only to come back and lead us to it again through more signs and disasters, by an even more circuitous and picturesque route. Opinions differ as to what John had in mind. One possibility is that his repetition adds nothing of substance, but is the equivalent of variations on a theme in music. The other main possibility is that in tantalisingly putting off reaching his climax he is indicating that God himself is continually putting off the day of judgement and sentence in order to give sinners more time to reconsider and repent.

The omission of the future tense from God in 11:17 may be a way of indicating that the end has come. 11:18 is a comment on the end in terms of Psalm 2. Christ, through his own death, through the witness of his martyrs and disciples and through the faithfulness of those they lead to repentance, defeats 'the destroyers of the earth'. By these 'destroyers', the forces of evil, John probably means what Eph 6:12 calls them: 'cosmic powers . . . the authorities and potentates of this dark world . . . the superhuman forces of evil in the heavens' (NEB).

11:19 is best taken with ch 12.

1. John has now given us four whole chapters of plagues and calamities. (There are more to come.) Is he guilty of pointless repetition?

2. Chapter 11 in particular, and much of Revelation in general, is incomprehensible to anyone ignorant of the OT. Ought christians today to make themselves familiar with the OT, or do we accept that Revelation remains a closed book for all but a few?

Rev 11:19. There was a Jewish tradition (2 Mac 2) that when the messiah came the long-lost ark of the covenant would reappear. It reappears now, with phenomena associated since Exodus with the appearing of God.

Rev 12:1–6. This is a heavenly representation of what is happening on earth, the conflict of the church with evil. (Chapters 12–14 are in many ways the heart and centre of the book of Revelation.) The woman stands for the people of God, which bore the messiah. The child is the messiah, crucified and glorified (12:5). The dragon is the symbol of evil pictured in terms of Daniel's apocalypse, in which many-headed and many-horned beasts stand for the persecuting empires of his time. For the evil persecution period of three years and a half the woman (the church) is exposed to terrible danger, and yet also, in the exodus wilderness, protected from it.

Rev 12:7–12. This is a separate scene picturing the dragon's defeat in other terms. His opponent now is the archangel Michael, the heavenly protagonist of God's people on earth. The pre-christian material of 12:7–9 is given a christian interpretation in 12:10–12. Through Christ and his martyrs, victory is won, and ascribed to Michael. The downfall of the devil to earth supplies an intelligible explanation of the terrible convulsions of evil before the end.

Rev 12:13–17. This takes up the scene of 12:1–6. The woman is given an eagle's wings (Ex 19:4) to escape the dragon, which tries to engulf her in the evil watery chaos of his own natural habitat. (12:16 may allude to Num 16:33 where the earth opened and swallowed up rebels against Moses.) The dragon makes war as best he can on the church (the woman's offspring or seed) and finally stands on the sea-shore calling up reinforcements.

The Jerusalem Bible notes that in this chapter 'it does not seem probable that John has Mary in mind or intended any allusion to the physical birth of the Messiah in the incarnation.' This is the common opinion of biblical scholars now, as it was of the early commentators. On the other hand, from the middle ages the woman was commonly identified with Mary the mother of Jesus. The JB leaves open the possibility that John had Mary too in mind, as the member of the people of God who in fact gave birth to Christ, and became the 'mother of the church' (a title given her by Pope Paul VI in 1964).

If John intended in this chapter no direct reference to Mary, is it in order for the church in later times to see one? Is there development in interpretation?

Rev 13:1–10. The next sign is a beast (already mentioned in passing at 11:7). John's one beast has the features of all Daniel's four, since there is now one Roman empire and the four empires known to Daniel are no more. To the Roman empire, which comes to Asia Minor over the sea, the dragon (Satan) delegates his power. Though John does not use the term in Revelation, the beast is antichrist, so the mortal wound may be a parody of the lamb's wounds; or it may be a reference to the suicide of Nero in 68 which was potentially a mortal wound to the whole Roman system. The beast demands worship and receives it from all except Christ's disciples. 13:9–10 may be a threat of divine retribution on the persecuting imperial power; alternatively, it may be a call to non-resistance, or to non-violent resistance, on the part of christians. The context in Jeremiah of the quotation in 13:10 favours the first interpretation; the comment about endurance and faith favours the second.

Rev 13:11–18. After the dragon (Satan) and the first beast (Rome), a second beast now appears, this time from the dry land. This third creature is later called the false prophet (spokesman) of the first beast and works in close collusion with it, securing for it worship from the world. The Jerusalem Bible notes that the three creatures of 12–13 may be intended as a dreadful parody of the Trinity.

The second beast seems to represent the local imperial government in Asia Minor and the East. (Much of the initiative towards Caesar-worship came from the East.) Caesar-worship was promoted in Asia Minor not only by legal coercion but also by fraud, ventriloquism, and social and economic discrimination. 13:17 may refer simply to the emperor's head on the coinage.

Numbers, in the classical world before arabic numerals, could only be written by means of letters of the alphabet. The number in 13:18 suggests that the name of the (first) beast was Nero, because Nero Caesar written in Hebrew letters is 666, and in Latin 616 (the variant reading in the Greek). The name of Jesus corresponded to 888; perfection was 777; all imperfection could be suggested by 666.

Some scholars think 13:17(b)–18 is an interpolation into John's work by some later editor. The passage is clumsily placed—it refers to the sea beast, and yet is placed after the description of the land beast. And it departs from John's usual theological style in the direction of some Jewish apocalyptic writing, which tends to treat visions as messages which if decoded yield hidden data about details of human history.

Rev 14:1–5. Now a sign in abrupt and total contrast. From those bearing the mark of the beast, John turns to those bearing the mark of the lamb. Their new song of praise is only to be known and sung by those who have persevered through persecution and suffering.

There are at least four possible ways to understand 14:4a which at first sight makes John look like a manichean. (1) The OT often used virginity and chastity as metaphors for faithfulness and true worship and commitment, just as conversely it often uses adultery and prostitution to signify idolatry and the pursuit of false values. St Paul speaks of the Corinthian church as a pure bride or chaste virgin in this sense (2 Cor 11:2), using the same Greek word *parthenos* for 'virgin' or 'chaste'. So John could be speaking of the 144,000 as the church, faithful to its calling. (2) Israel's rules for holy war against enemies said that fighting men who had intercourse with their wives during war incurred ritual defilement (see the story of David and Uriah, 2 Sam 11:11). So John may be presenting the church as faithful in its holy war. (3) Possibly John is thinking of the heavenly life where 'they neither marry nor are given in marriage' (Mk 12:25). (4) Possibly John is thinking of male celibates as the normal membership of the church. There is a little evidence from the East in early centuries of churches in which baptism was given only to the deeply committed, and in which ordinary believers were catechumens.

Any literal understanding of the passage tends to cast a doubt on the institution of marriage, which the church values and blesses (even declaring heretical those manicheans and dualists who disparaged it). So most commentators have favoured a metaphorical interpretation. If we join them, though, we ought to be ready with an answer to a question which keeps recurring: Why does the church take *parthenos* literally and physically in connection with Mary (Mt 1, Lk 1, the creeds) but (as a rule) metaphorically in Revelation? The usual explanation is reached by making a distinction between historical prose and apocalyptic poetry.

Rev 14:6–13. Another sign, consisting of three angelic proclamations.

(1) 'An eternal gospel' is a strange phrase. (It led Joachim of Fiore in the twelfth century to teach that a third revelation, an age of the Spirit, would come and supersede the OT, the age of the Father, and the NT, the age of the Son.) Probably John means the gospel conceived in eternity though revealed in time. The gospel is a call to repentance. The unbelieving world still has value in God's eyes: it is not rejected in advance, but called to turn to the truth.

(2) Christ's victory has already meant the downfall of 'Babylon'—Rome—which imposed idolatry by law.

(3) Those who comply with this Roman law will suffer the torments of the damned (the language is Isaiah's).

The meaning of 14:12 is that the wrath of God is an incentive to christians to endure, or (and?) that christians must continue bearing witness in the hope that the world may yet repent.

Rev 14:14–20. Another sign: the judgement as a harvesting. In Matthew's parable of the weeds sown among the wheat, 'the harvest is the close of the age, and the reapers are angels' (Mt 13:39). In this sign there are two harvestings. The first may be the saving harvest of the just, and the second the destructive harvest of the rejected. Or it is all one harvest of both just and rejected viewed as twofold because the general experience of men was of a twofold earthly harvest—of corn (the harvest proper) and of fruit (the vintage).

What do you think is the most satisfactory explanation of 14 : 4?

Rev 15 : 1–8. This chapter draws a parallel between the events of the exodus and the events before the end. John still proceeds from the known to the unknown. To the ten plagues of the exodus story correspond seven of Revelation: to the sea of reeds, a sea of glass; to the pillar of fire, the fire in the sea; to Israel, the conquerors; to Pharaoh's tyranny, Rome's; to the song of Moses, a new song; to the wilderness tent, the heavenly tent; and to the priests of Israel's worship, the seven angels carrying out an eschatological liturgy.

Rev 16 : 1–21. John goes over the old ground yet again. These plagues, like the exodus plagues, are intended to soften hearts and lead men to repent, as well as to punish the unrepentant who harden their hearts. Repentance is still a possibility after the fifth plague.

In this series, the plagues are very explicitly directed towards those who promote emperor-worship and persecute the church. In the squalid picture of 16 : 13–14 (still related, through the frogs, to the exodus) it seems that demonic forces from within the three creatures, which are by now closely identified with Rome, go and gather Rome's enemies for battle against the empire. The great military confrontation is envisaged at Armageddon, a mythical site related to the field of Megiddo, the prototype for Israel of all fateful battlefields.

The pouring of the seventh bowl spells the destruction of Rome, which John describes in highly apocalyptic imagery.

What, if anything, distinguishes the sevenfold series in ch 16 from those in chs 6, 8, and 9?

3

The fall of Rome and the defeat of evil
Rev 17:1–20:15

Rev 17:1–6. Chapter 16 was unusually specific about Rome as the source of evil. Chapters 17–20 now portray in detail, for the encouragement of the church, the violent downfall of the Roman empire. (Though we are shown the destruction of Rome only indirectly, through the eyes of horrified onlookers.)

The harlot is 'Babylon'—Rome. The many waters are the Euphrates and the irrigation canals where Babylon stood, and the sea (haunt of the beast) over which Roman power came, colonising everywhere. The key to the repulsive description is the abominations or obscenities (17:4). The Greek word is the one used at Mk 13:14 and Dan 12:11, where it denotes the desecrating sacrilege of heathen idolatry forcibly intruded into the holy place of the temple. The harlot symbolises all idolatry, all false values, all wrong-doing.

Rev 17:7–8. After the vision, an interpretation. The beast, was, is not, and is to come—another parody of God. Either Nero is meant, who lived and died and was popularly expected to return to life; or Rome is meant which persecuted actively under Nero, then desisted, and then persecuted again under Domitian.

Rev 17:9–18. Here one could wish the angel had explained more clearly. Arguably, 17:9–17 is a secondary reinterpretation inserted into John's text by a later editor. The reasons for thinking so are these. The unusually lengthy explanation gives a double interpretation: the seven heads of the beast are the seven hills, *and* seven emperors. The passage includes a further victory of the lamb, over and above his passion and glorification, which is out of step with the theology of Revelation as a whole (see 5:5). And in 17:10–11 we seem to have the Jewish apocalyptic device of pretending to stand in the past and thence to predict future events which in fact are within the writer's experience. And there is deep obscurity in 17:12–17, where the straight conflict of the harlot with the lamb is complicated by a conflict between Rome and her subject peoples—after their defeat. For all these reasons, it may be best to put brackets round 17:10–17, as the probable interpolation of a commentator. The basis of what we are being told, whether by John or another, is that a series of seven emperors symbolise Rome's corruption, that another (Domitian?) will soon follow as an eighth in line, that he will be the persecuting beast or antichrist, and that therefore the end is near and christians may have high hope. The passage has led people to try to identify the seven emperors, but no one has ever given a convincing list, and probably the seven is a purely symbolic number.

Rev 18:1–24. A prominent feature of OT prophecy is the 'oracle against foreign nations'—the denunciation, lamentation, or taunt-song describing the dreadful destruction of some enemy of Israel and of God for false worship and morality. In this chapter John draws on material used by Isaiah and Ezekiel against the city of Tyre and by Jeremiah against Babylon, to express the imminent annihilation of Rome. John shows us this, not directly, but through the contrasting reactions to it of the world and of the church.

A new theme comes into the foreground. This is the *wealth* of Rome, its predatory commercialism, its exploitation of its colonies, its attractiveness to profiteers and seekers after luxurious living. For this theme, although he continues calling Rome Babylon, John uses OT passages which are denunciations of the Phoenician trading city of Tyre.

From Tyre, into Israel, had come Jezebel, introducing among God's people horrifying baal worship and equally horrifying free enterprise economics (see the story of Elijah). The earlier, traditional, socio-economic organisation of Israel aimed at the general welfare of the people as a whole. In so far as Israel tried to keep the land evenly distributed among families, her system was relatively egalitarian, and the prophets never doubted that extremes of wealth and poverty were against God's will. For a picture of the head-on collision of the differing economic outlooks of Israel and Phoenicia, see the story of Naboth's vineyard in 1 Kg 21. These are the themes of socio-economic morality which John takes up and applies to the Roman empire.

1. Revelation shows us christians in opposition to the prevailing social, economic and political order. Christians today are not required to worship heads of governments, but in many places they are required as citizens to share responsibility for wars, war preparations, extremes of wealth and poverty, and racial and ideological discrimination. Are they right if in these circumstances they live at peace with society?

2. In fact Rome did not fall. The church eventually

converted the harlot to her own faith. (Or did Rome convert the church?) Either way, what about John as a prophet?

3. *Is this chapter exultantly vindictive (see 18:6–7, 20)? If so, does it detract from the character of Revelation as a christian book?*

4. *'Religion is a way of legitimising the ruling power'. How does this popular marxist theory of religion look in the light of the book of Revelation?*

Rev 19:1–10. Following the vision of the annihilation of Rome and the lamentation of the harlot's devotees, comes a counterpart vision of the church, the bride, rejoicing, united to the lamb at the eschatological banquet.

The first part of 19:10 may be an aside against angel-worship, of which there is some evidence in the NT (Col 2:18), or a warning against a subtle form of idolatry. The last sentence of 19:10 is unclear: it seems to mean that the word of God as revealed in Jesus is present through the Spirit in the prophets of the church.

Rev 19:11–16. Now John takes a step away from local happenings in recognisably historical time, towards the final universal events outside time. These are the parousia and judgement (19–20) and the new creation (21–22)—the eschatological events which are not only future but also present, within time, for the believer.

Christ appears as eschatological ruler: the horse he rides is white for victory and holiness, and where a warrior's sword would be, he wears the title of lord of all. 'Faithful and true', he is utterly to be relied upon: all who have put their faith in him will turn out to have been right. His eyes are those of the Son of God (2:18). The mystery of his divinity prevents men naming him adequately, but as God's word, he embodies revelation in his person.

Rev 19:17–21. 'He judges and makes war.' John pictures the judgement of the rejected in a counterpart vision corresponding to the lamb's marriage-supper. The macabre meal is in terms borrowed with little adaptation from Ez 39:17–20. Though there is a great gathering as if for battle, there is no battle. The victory of Christ was won long ago, at Calvary. The beast and its accomplice and all the enemy forces are rendered powerless without a struggle. The followers of the beasts die by the sword, and the beasts themselves are consigned to the lake of fire that burns for ever.

From one point of view, this vision describes no new event; it merely discloses what has already taken place and is known through faith. All that happens now is that the lights are turned on.

Rev 20:1–15. To take the whole chapter quite literally, first of all. Unlike the other two monsters already in the burning lake, the dragon (Satan) is chained in the bottomless pit for a thousand years. Meanwhile the martyrs and other faithful christians rise to new life in a first resurrection and reign with Christ for a thousand years in a world still peopled by the pagan nations, who are still vulnerable to the deceptions of Satan. (Though the Greek at 20:4 is rather loose, it is probable that John distinguishes two categories, the martyrs, and those who had not worshipped the beast. RSV and NEB choose to understand only one group, the martyrs.) At the end of the millennium, Satan is loosed for a time, but defeated and consigned to the burning lake. The rest of the dead are then judged and the wicked thrown into the burning lake, the 'second death'. Then death and Hades are themselves destroyed, and earth and sky vanish to make room for a new creation (21 : 1). How is this rather unexpected chapter to be understood?

Rev 20 : 1–6. The chief puzzle is how to understand the millennium—the reign of the just with Christ for a thousand years on this earth—and the release of Satan to do damage afterwards.

One suggestion is that John wanted to find room in his work for all the traditions he found in his sources, and did not entirely harmonise them all with his work as a whole. In the prophets and in the OT generally, the hope is expressed that the coming of the messiah would mean an ideal human life lived in this terrestrial world renewed and transformed. (See for example, Is 65 : 17–25.) And a belief in a messianic reign for a period of years is found in some non-canonical apocalypses, such as 4 Ezra.

Continuity with tradition may be part of the explanation, but we have to assume that John introduces the millennium deliberately, gives it a meaning consistent with Revelation as a whole, and intends his readers to take it seriously. So the suggestion is that the millennium must in some way stand for the life of the church between Christ's resurrection and his parousia.

Adopting this suggestion, some have taken a literal approach. Montanus waited at Pepuza for the new Jerusalem to descend. Respected theologians of the early church like St Justin and St Irenaeus expected a thousand-year reign of Christ before the end. Joachim of Fiore in the twelfth century used Rev 20 as a foundation of his teaching about the coming 'spiritual church'. In 1534–5 some Anabaptists took control of the city of Münster and tried to inaugurate the millennial kingdom of the saints by political action, proclaiming John of Leyden King of New Zion, and decreeing the common ownership of all goods. This millenarian theology has been kept alive in some modern adventist sects, and (in a secularised form) in some utopian political movements.

Others, particularly since St Augustine (c 400), have understood the millennium as the life of the church on earth in a less literal way. Today it is quite commonly held that it is wrong to take the thousand years literally as any stretch of historical time at all. As usual in Revelation, the number is a symbol. The evil three and a half years stood for persecution. Probably the millennium is the exact counterpart—the ideal limitless period of the church's real (but so far hidden) triumph, concurrent with persecution. In fact, the millennium would stand for the one, timeless, moment of the end. And probably the point John wants to make lies beyond such puzzles about the time factor. His point is that the truth about Christ and the world, now hidden except to the eyes of faith, will soon be visible to all in the public order of things.

Rev 20:7–10. In an explanation along these lines, the 'loosing of Satan' is intelligible. As the positive side of Christ's victory is unveiled, so is the negative. Satan is exhibited, like a beast in an arena, solely in order that he may be seen to be powerless, and destroyed. Though the armies of the pagan nations assemble (in spite of their elimination in 19:21), Satan can make no effective resistance and can do no further damage. His power, towards the end, is only one of deceiving—pretending to the unbelievers that Christ's victory has not happened, that evil is still dominant, and that the apparent surface order of things is the real one. Now, even this power is at an end, because Christ's victory is soon to be unmistakably clear for all to see. (And therefore let no christian give way, and worship the emperor.)

Rev 20:11–15. John depicts the last judgement simply and briefly. The decisive question is, do you belong to Christ? The book of life is the book of life of the lamb, as 13:8 calls it.

1. 'Every mob-leader's bag of tricks.' What is there in Revelation to explain this description of the book, by Luther?

2. What problems arise for the rest of scripture and for christian belief if Rev 20 is taken literally? What problems arise if it is not taken literally?

4

The new Jerusalem
Rev 21:1–22:21

Rev 21:1–8. The millennial kingdom was on this earth. The final kingdom is a new creation which comes to this world from God.

At a deep level, John is concerned with the theological problem of continuity and discontinuity. On the one hand, John's new creation is radically new. It does not renew the old: it replaces it. On the other hand, his symbol of the new creation is still Jerusalem, and this section is more than ever a composition of OT passages.

John does not answer directly the question we may be tempted to ask: is the 'next world' or 'everlasting life' the life of this universe evolved to a consummation or omega point, or is it located altogether elsewhere? John was aware of the alternatives. Much OT prophecy, convinced of the basic goodness of creation, favoured the first answer; much apocalyptic writing, convinced of the irremediable evil of this world, favoured the second.

John does not answer this problem directly, but in showing heaven and earth at the end no longer separate but united, his vision suggests one way to a solution. 'The dwelling of God is with man.' God 'tents' with men, as the Word dwelt with us at the incarnation (Jn 1:14). (This question of continuity or discontinuity bears some relation to the medieval discussions of nature and grace, and to the modern question whether or not christians are called, as the church, to political and social activity.)

Note in 21:5–8 the only words in all Revelation which are attributed to God himself in the first person. The passage must be meant to carry a heavy weight of emphasis. What do we find, so strongly stressed? We find an echo of the letters to the seven churches. We find again the promise of reward for the victorious martyr, and a corresponding warning that the cowardly who fail to measure up to the challenge of persecution will be consigned with other sinners to everlasting death.

Rev 21:9–27. Though John is describing a city, he is really concerned with new relationships, of God with man, and man with man. The 'bride', the 'wife of the lamb' is God's people. The vision of the bride is probably a deliberate counterpart of the vision of the harlot in ch 17).

The city descends at 21:2, and again at 21:10. For those who tend to take John literally and adopt a futuristic eschatology, John is going back to give a more detailed account of the same vision. For those who take John non-literally and adopt a realised eschatology, there is no problem: the holy city—Christ—comes continually.

The city has a wall, and there are still outsiders (21:8; 21:27). In one way, John suggests that rejection as well as salvation is an eschatological reality. Yet at the same time the city has gates, bearing the names of Israel's tribes, and the gates are open. John is urging the Jews to turn to the messiah and believe, and not only Jews but also pagans and the kings of the earth are still being called and invited in (21:24–26).

The measurements and ornamentation of the city evoke its magnificence and perfection. Perhaps it is a

cube because the holy of holies in Solomon's temple was
a cube.

The new city has no temple. This sets John's eschatology in marked contrast with most OT eschatology, and
in harmony with Jn 2:21 ('he spoke of the temple of his
body'). For Israel, the temple had been of prime importance as the place of God's presence and of the holy, as
distinct from all that was common and from the rest of
creation from which God was by implication absent. In
the new city the division between sacred and secular is
overcome. All is of God, except what remains actively
hostile to him, outside the wall.

*What position in his scheme of things does John give
to holy places?*

Rev 22:1–5. This section continues 21:9–27, but it is
also a separate vision, in that it presents the new creation
of ch 21—the new holy city, holy world, holy community
—in terms of the paradise garden. That John speaks of
'the healing of the nations' and the end of everything
accursed may suggest that he has hope and faith in the
ultimate repentance of 'those who dwell on the earth'—in
the universality of salvation. The vision of God leads
naturally to a mention of liturgical worship (22:3–4).
With God's name on their foreheads, they are irrevocably
his.

Rev 22:6–21. Here begins a sort of epilogue, in which
we are back in John's present, and Jesus, the angel and
John address concluding promises and warnings to the
churches. The Greek is indefinite enough for translations
to differ in the way they apportion the words to the
speakers, but a natural division (with the main points
made) seems to be as follows:

6   The angel: Revelation is to be relied on.

7   Jesus: Persevere, as Revelation directs, in the knowledge that he is coming.

8   John: The visions so overwhelmed him that he was tempted to worship the angel.

9–11   The angel: Such worship would be wrong. John's book is relevant *now* (unlike Daniel's which purported to have been sealed up for centuries till it became relevant). Judgement is now near, whatever men may choose to do.

12–13   Jesus: He is coming.

14–15   John: A blessing on the faithful, a lament on sinners. (Dogs: specifically in scripture male prostitutes, Deut 13:18; generally unclean outsiders, Mt 7:6.)

16   Jesus: (words like those to the seven churches).

17–21   John (himself, or quoting other voices): The Holy Spirit and the church are inviting christians forward to meet Christ in and through martyrdom. Revelation is reliable: 18–19 are a conventional apocalyptic warning. It may be a coincidence, but at 22:20 Jesus refers a *seventh* time to his coming. (2:5, 16; 3:11; 16:15; 22:7, 12, 20.) 'Come, Lord Jesus': at 1 Cor 16:22 the Greek original quotes the early christian liturgical prayer in Aramaic, *maran atha*, 'our Lord come'. This seems to be substantially the same prayer, and if so Revelation perhaps ends as it began, in the context of a liturgical celebration. 22:21 is the sort of conclusion found at the end of NT letters.

1. Is the message of Revelation useful for christians who live without any real prospect of martyrdom but with all the various testing trials short of martyrdom?

2. *Christians have on the whole rejected the biblical story of the creation of the world and of man as a factual account, while holding to belief in its theological teaching. Is there any reason why the biblical account of the end should continue to be accepted as factual?*

3. *Was John writing about the future with an eye on the present (mainly futurist eschatology), or about the present with an eye on the future (mainly realised eschatology)?*

4. *Is there a point towards the end of Revelation at which it is too late to repent?*

5. *'The joys and the hopes, the griefs and the anxieties of the men of this age, especially those who are poor or in any way afflicted, these too are the joys and hopes, the griefs and anxieties of the followers of Christ.' (Vatican II:* On the Church in the World Today, *§ 1.) Look at this proposition and at Revelation in the light of each other.*

6. *How should we use the book of Revelation today (if at all)? If you were asked, and agreed, to arrange a series of services based on the book, how would you go about it? (Try it in practice.)*